On Being
a Department Head
a Personal View

John B. Conway

American Mathematical Society

1991 *Mathematics Subject Classification.* Primary 00A20.

Library of Congress Cataloging-in-Publication Data

Conway, John B.
On being a department head, a personal view / John B. Conway.
p. cm.
ISBN 0-8218-0615-7 (alk. paper)
1. Departmental chairmen (Universities)—United States. 2. Universities and colleges—United States—Departments. 3. Mathematics—Study and teaching (Higher)—United States. I. Title.
LB2341.C7596   1996
378.1′11—dc20   96-22067
                                                                                                     CIP

For Ann,
my travelling and dining companion,
confidant, best friend, and lover

Contents

Preface

In many ways this book is as natural an outgrowth of my activities as writing a book on complex analysis. I did a great deal of work learning about the topic, and I felt I wanted to write the book that I wish had been available to me when I started my study. As I was contemplating becoming the head of a department, I would have profited from the kind of document I am writing now. It would certainly have been kept within easy reach during my first year as head, when I was cautiously feeling my way. Even as a graduate student I might have read a book like this, and I definitely would have as a new faculty member in my first department. I have always been curious how departments run, and I was never certain whether my department was typical or unusual.

As stated in the title, this book is a personal view of the office of head. Like everyone else, I am influenced by what has happened to me, what I have done, and what I have seen in my career as a faculty member and as a department head. I fervently believe that what I write about here applies to many other departments, not just my own. Yes, I will tell you many of the things I do as a a department head. No, this does not mean that I think you should do what I do.

If there is one thing I have learned as a department head, it is that problems connected with people seldom have unique solutions. Problems involving people, however, are uniquely defined by that person, the place where they are, and the time in which they live. So even though something works for me, it might not work for you. You might also solve a problem in a way that makes you feel more comfortable than anything I propose. Maybe your solution is better. Write me a letter or email; I'm interested.

When I discuss important topics like tenure, salaries, and recruiting, I'll present what I see as the difficulties, the important questions, and the potential hazards to a department head when (s)he makes a decision in such an arena. But I'll also tell you what I think is a good course of action. If you're looking for an objective presentation, you'll be disappointed. Besides a personal view of being a department head, this is an opinionated view. Disagree with me if you like. Curse me out if you must. But if more people think about the role of the head of a department, I believe the entire profession will profit.

I think it might be helpful for other heads as well as faculty members to read the opinions, observations, and advice of one head. From all the comments I have heard over the years about department heads, much of which was nonsense, I think most rank-and-file faculty can get something from what I have written. University faculty, moreover, must begin to be more savvy in the world of academic politics.

The economy and the political scene have undergone enormous change. Industry is downsizing and many are losing their jobs and, at best, finding new employment at greatly reduced incomes. The entire base of the economy is shifting. Frustration and anxiety are apparent in the rise of radical political movements. In such an atmosphere can anyone believe that any part of society will remain unchanged? Society is an ecological system and change in any part of it will produce change in its entirety.

But in their actions faculty often seem not to realize this or, at least, to act as though it isn't so. Clearly they wish it weren't so. In fact, what happens in the university always seems to lag behind what is happening outside. But the dreaded downsizing has begun in academia. We are beginning to feel some of the same forces that have beguiled and disrupted the lives of factory workers for many years. We had better learn to cope.

The enormous crunch towards formalized assessment and accountability is beginning to affect us all. We have always been held accountable, but today the parameters have changed. Increasingly, often with the cooperation of university administrators, we are being asked to live by the same rules that govern business. This will have a far more permanent effect than importing a flock of Russian and East European mathematicians and scientists.

For years higher education prospered. It loudly proclaimed that college graduates command far greater lifetime incomes. Ample funding followed. We produced. But that argument has begun to sour. A college degree has long since stopped being a guarantee of prosperity or even job security. Society has begun to question its support of universities. In this environment mathematicians and all academics must begin to change, compete, and seek resorces that will be used with greater care. It is the only solution if we hope to maintain the integrity of the enterprise.

Essential in this is the role of administrators in the university. From the university president on down to the department head, college faculty should insist that its leaders be strong scholars if there is any hope of having the value of research and scholarship properly represented. A key to this entire undertaking is the department head, and essential to his/her success is the understanding by the faculty of the role of the head.

Am I an expert on being a department head? Of course not. In fact, after six years of searching, I haven't found any experts. I do have some credentials that justify my writing this book and might warrant your time in reading it. I have been a head for 6 years now and I was a faculty member for 25 years before that. During that 25-year stretch, I was in a department that had an election for chair every three years and chairs were not allowed to succeed themselves. Under this system I got to see a lot of different styles. I also try to be an observant person and have some sensitivity to the world around me.

Another part of my background that contributes to my credentials for writing this book is that since I became a head I have consciously set about to study the job. Part of my routine is an internal debriefing at the end of the day, usually as I take a walk before dinner. When I visit another department I invariably schedule an appointment to meet my counterpart and learn how they approach their job. In fact, since I became a head I have used every opportunity presented me to learn what others do as heads. Initially I did this to learn how to do my job better. With time, the idea of writing this book took shape and seeking out other heads became a part of the reason for accepting a speaking invitation. It didn't take long to realize that heads face many of the same problems, no matter the type or size of the department.

Now some nomenclature. Is it Head? Chair? Chairperson? What's in a name? I really don't care what you call the position, but for some academics the term "head" seems to have a meaning distinct from that of "chair". They refer to a "head" as someone who has a great deal of central authority and a "chair" as someone who is at the head of a democratized unit. My position is more like the former, and it is explicitly stated in our bylaws that all votes are advisory to the head.

I lived most of my academic life under a "chair" system. This heavily democratized system from my former life supplanted a loosely democratized one that had been abused. I was never chair in that system. In my estimation the system with less democracy is better, in spite of the possibility of abuse. But this may be the view from my present vantage point. On the other hand, my endorsement of a democratically run department had its global maximum when I was a very young assistant professor. My opinion of the value of democracy in the running of an academic department has been monotonically decreasing throughout my career.

But here is the fundamental rule. The head who acts more like a chair and the chair who acts more like a head will be more successful than one who tries to live in a pure state. So in this book I am not going to maintain a distinction. I think that what I have to say applies to both circumstances.

I will almost always use the term "head" rather than "chair". I like the title because in academic circles "chair" is ambiguous. It is often used as in the "Chair in Analysis" or the "Bovid Chair". I also do not like the term "chairperson". I appreciate the sensitivities of my female colleagues and see many good reasons to adopt sexless nomenclature. I do this willingly and gladly. But "chairperson" is offensive to my sensitivity about language. (It especially grates when I hear someone refer to a person as the "chairperson" when the person referred to has a well defined and readily identifiable sex.)

So, gentle reader, the term "head" will be used with no attached subtle meaning. It simply refers to the person in charge of the department, regardless of the style of governance.

I also have to say that I have considerably less knowledge of the workings of departments that are very small, those at community colleges, or even those at what are primarily teaching universities. I have visited such places and talked with their heads, and I have participated in meetings with both faculty and heads of such departments. Nevertheless, some of what is here will not apply to certain departments. That probably did not need to be stated.

One more word about late-breaking events. As I finished the manuscript for this book, events at the University of Rochester came to a head, and the administration there decided to terminate their PhD program in mathematics. The American Mathematical Society sent a team to discuss matters with the university, and the Council of the American Mathematical Society passed a resolution expressing their disapproval. Eventually, the PhD program in mathematics was reinstated. How did these events affect this book?

I added §28, "Relations with other departments"; I should have had such a section independent of Rochester. But I am neither a participant nor a first-hand observer of the scene there. I also think it would be a mistake to fasten on the "problem of the moment" in mathematics. I think there are things for all of us to learn from that situation. One, certainly, is the fragility of academic existence. Another is that we have to nurture many aspects of our role in a university. Some of this is discussed specifically in §28, but it is a theme that runs throughout the book. As time goes on we'll undoubtedly learn more.

I have profited from the comments of several colleagues who generously agreed to read earlier versions of this book. Hank Frandsen, Wanda Giles, and Jerzy Dydak made several suggestions, some followed, some not, but all helpful for their different points of view. My wife, Ann, read the first draft as well as a later version. She probably helped me avoid more controversy than I wanted. I embrace and am responsible for whatever controversy and outrageous expressions remain.

A word about one aspect of the writing style in this book which I believe violates some of the usual advice to authors. Often I will write as though I were talking to another department head. (For example, "You ought to run a tight ship.") At other times I'll write in the third person. ("Department heads should run a tight ship.") Still other times I'll tell you something about myself. ("I believe in running a tight ship. But my definition of a tight ship may be different from that of many others.") The purpose of this document is manifold. I want to offer advice to department heads out there. I want to try to educate the rank and file about a variety of aspects of the job of being a department head. I also want to tell you my opinion about this job and perhaps also a little about love, death, and the vagaries of the human condition.

Contemplating the Prospect of Being a Head

§1. What does it take to be a department head?

In keeping with my prior disclaimer of expertise, I really don't know the answer to this. I'm not sure there is a set answer in the usual sense. I've known many people at my own institutions as well as others who have totally different personalities, psyches, degrees of organization, and levels of mathematical ability but would do or have done a good job of being a head. I've also known some successful heads and some failures who have many similarities. I have also seen some people fail at the job who I thought would be successful. It's hard to predict and surely depends as much on the department as on the individual.

It's rather clear that a department head should be organized, fair, honest, and open minded. I also think a department head should be an optimist; some might think I am being facetious by saying that, but I am totally serious. It is inevitable that every department will have hard times. You, as a head, must believe that, with work, problems will be solved or at least ameliorated.

Rather that generating a list of desirable traits for the job, let me make some statements that I think a good prospect for a head should agree with. Then I'll make a few I think they should disagree with.

1. Usually at the end of the day I can remember where I parked my car.
2. There are some issues in mathematics that I care a lot about, and there are others on which I am neutral. I have never ceased to be amazed that there are some mathematicians who seem to be passionate about everything.
3. I like people. I think it is interesting to observe how people act and react.
4. Vanilla is not my favorite flavor.
5. Being a department head is an important job. There is a lot to do, and the head's decisions have important consequences.

1

6. Being a dean is an important job. There is a lot to do, and the dean's decisions have important consequences.

7. Disagreeing with someone does not cause me to lose respect for them. I've heard some crazy opinions expressed in my life, and I wonder about the holder's sanity. But most of the time I just see different opinions as the result of someone starting with the same facts but attaching different weights to these facts and using an alternate, but valid, reasoning process. I can still respect them even though I think they are wrong.

8. Logical consistency does not imply truth. Just because I discover a scenario that explains all the known facts does not mean I have discovered the truth. There may be facts that I don't know, and, even if I do, valid explanations are not unique.

9. Mathematics is a great profession, and there is room in it for people of vastly different levels of talent.

10. It is important to lead people toward worthy goals. Some objectives, however, are so important that if people won't be led there, they have to be pushed.

Now for some statements a prospective head should disagree with.

1. Being the head of the department is basically a social position. This is the person who the department designates to have dinner with the dean, meet parents of prospective students, and administer the secretarial staff. (This was said by a junior colleague many years ago.)

2. Mathematicians behave differently than other people.

3. All people are basically good, and with the right approach they will always do what is best for the common good.

4. No action should be taken unless at least two-thirds of the faculty agree.

5. The only good dean is an invisible one.

6. Most departments run themselves.

7. My scholarly life is over.

8. The most important part of my day is my noontime run.

9. The least important part of my day is my noontime run.

10. Secretaries ought to be quiet and do what they are told.

11. Faculty ought to be quiet and do what they are told.

12. All human difficulties can be resolved to everyone's satisfaction.

§2. Interviewing for the job.

There are two possibilities here, of course. You could be interviewing for the job as head at your current university, or you could be a candidate at a different institution. I have never had the former experience, but I have had the latter more than once. There are some things that are common to both situations and call for similar approaches; other factors and questions are pertinent to only one of these. There are issues here that will affect you personally and those that will concern the future of the department you are about to take over.

I am not one to get involved in some of the game playing that you occasionally hear about. In fact, I wonder how much of this really goes on. Remember that you will be living with this dean afterwards. If you lie or cheat or if (s)he even believes that you have, (s)he is going to remember it, and it is likely (s)he will exact some form of payment. Unless, of course, the dean is a saint (and, like department heads, no dean is a saint). You may not get a raise, the department may not get its share of resources. So be honest and forthright. This is not to say you should reveal all. Remember, this is a negotiation, not a group therapy session.

Before you start the interview process, there are a couple of questions you should ask yourself. How much do you want this job? How much does the dean want you for the job? Clearly the answers will determine how stubborn you will be and how quickly or slowly you can anticipate the dean will respond.

I think it is a mistake to go into the negotiations with a long shopping list. Decide what's important and how important it is. Be aware of the difference between recurring and non-recurring budget items. Deans are usually much more receptive to a request that will be taken care of in a single year rather that an obligation that is eternal. So $30,000 of computers may be more likely to be given than an annual increase of $5,000 in the travel fund.

As in all things, you should do your homework. Do you really think that the dean is going to agree to an extra two faculty positions simply because you ask for them? Maybe you are such a hot commodity that you'll get this. Maybe not. Maybe there is a recent review of the department that shows that in the past 5 years the number of mathematics majors at this university has increased by 30% with no increase in faculty. You can't hire people with masters degrees to teach juniors and seniors. This is the kind of thing deans listen to. By the way, it is important to realize that deans are intelligent. They will laugh at you and lose respect for you if you tell them you need research faculty because the enrollment in precalculus has increased.

Of course if you are an external candidate, it is unlikely you can make a case for additional faculty, travel funds, operating budget with the kind of specificity that deans (or anyone who controls a budget) listen to. What do you really know about the department? You have heard the complaints during your visit, but the dean has also heard these. Did the people there give you ammunition? If so, use it. But do you really want to go to the wall on this when what you have is second-hand information? How important is the issue to you and the department?

I can be a rather good salesman, but only when I am convinced that what I am selling is good. I think it would be very hard to sell the dean during an interview when all I have is information gathered over a few days or weeks preceding the interview. If you are an external candidate, you are likely to be one of several and, therefore, not fully briefed on the dominant issues in the department. An internal candidate, on the other hand, has a distinct advantage here. Not only will (s)he have all the information available, but it may be that (s)he is the only candidate or just one of two. In this situation, selling a plan at the outset is a possibility. At least it is much more likely that the presentation can be carried off with credibility.

Obtaining new positions is certainly the most glamorous part of the whole process. With reason! When you step down, the judgment of your career as head will be based largely on how well you recruited. There are other things that can land you in the Heads' Hall of Fame, like 10 years of departmental tranquility or the quintessential major program. Small colleges tend to have more stable faculty, and hiring is probably not so dominant in determining the success of a head at such an institution. But even here, when there is the opportunity to recruit, it is your chance to blossom or wither. Just about every department I know feels it is understaffed (maybe they are). Bringing new positions into the department as your maiden act certainly sends the message that you are effective and gives your faculty a belief that you are going to be successful. But I have heard of very few heads that took over with a commitment of a large number of positions. In these days of tight budgets, it will become even more rare.

Unless there is a very unusual set of circumstances, I think it unwise to make additional positions the *sine qua non* of your acceptance. But it isn't too hard to imagine conditions where this is a reasonable stance. For example, suppose you are happy in your present position and the university that is courting you is weak. The only appeal of accepting the headship (aside from the beautiful view of the ocean) is the possibility of launching an adventure and creating the world's center for the study of quasi-barrelled locally convex spaces. Then by all means, let the dean know that you aren't interested in the job unless it is accompanied by new positions. But don't exaggerate. Say what you mean, mean what you say. (Good advice when buying a car as well as negotiating for a headship.)

I think it is more important to assess attitudes than get firm commitments. What will it take for the department to get an additional position, another computer lab, an additional secretary, or whatever it is that will boost morale or increase departmental prestige? Is the dean someone who is reasonable and likely to respond to a careful argument that demonstrates the problem? Is the university expanding? Contracting? Does the college administration think the department's main role is servicing other programs, or does the dean have a respect for mathematics as an independent discipline? These are much more important questions than whether you will get a specific request. I can almost guarantee that three years after you take office what you think is important for the department is not what you thought when you started.

In §11 I discuss the salary question, but here are a few reasonable ideas about money. If you are a candidate from the outside, I think you should be able to expect a significant raise — something on the order of 1 to 2 months of your present salary. You should also make sure you are paid something significant during the summer, probably another month's salary or so. (Two additional paychecks during the summer essentially gives you a 12-month contract. I'll say something about this idea shortly.) Perhaps in a small department these numbers are high, especially the latter one since small departments in liberal arts colleges seldom have the extensive summer school programs that the large state universities do. Summer school is a rather quiet affair; but even if you are not going to be heavily involved in the day-to-day operation, you should be paid a significant amount. Here's why.

At most institutions the summer budget is a separate entity from that of the academic year. While the academic year budget may be quite tight, summer budgets tend to have more roominess. Summer school is a money-making proposition for most universities because summer salaries are low relative to the amount of credit hours generated. This is especially true of mathematics departments. Also the basic upkeep of the buildings and the pay for the support staff is already taken care of by the general fund. So a dean is more likely to be able to dip into the summer budget to reward you than to pay you a big academic year salary. Be careful though. The dean may not have much control over the summer school budget; chancellors, provosts, and presidents know a good thing when they see it. Also some schools do not pay fringe benefits on summer school salaries; in that case it may take $1.30 in the summer to equal a dollar in the academic year.

If you have been active in research, getting grants on a regular basis, that may not be the case after you become a head. If you are conscientious about the job, you may not have as much time for your own research as you formerly did. Grant money may disappear. There is also an assumption that department heads disengage from research (more on that later), and a granting agency and your peer evaluators may look at you differently than before you became an administrator. So get a little income during the summer so that that raise you got doesn't evaporate if you lose the grant. And keep the formal duties that are required of you during the summer to a minimum so you can use the extra time you have for research and scholarship. You need it, and it's important for your success both as a mathematician and as a head.

There is also the possibility of trying for a 12-month appointment. This isn't impossible. I don't know how many have this. It sounds good; after all, suppose you add N kilobucks to your academic salary and then give yourself three additional paychecks. This is serious money. There may be a price to pay, however. This really puts you in the category of "administrator". Are you ready for it? It will be harder to return to the faculty in the future; like most human beings you will become accustomed to those three extra checks and will feel it if you have to give them up. Also, if you have a research or educational grant, it is likely to be the case that you will not be able to have the grant pay you a summer salary. Finally 12-month appointments have rules attached to them that faculty members are not used to. You have to more closely account for your time, the number of holidays is prescribed, etc. If you want to stay home and work in private on your latest book, that may not be possible unless you use one of your holidays.

If you are an internal candidate, you probably have less flexibility, but I suspect there are wide local variations. What has happened in the past? How large is your current salary relative to your local peers? If I were a dean and I was discussing salary with a head who was only going to be in office for 3 years, I would be reluctant to give a big raise. I think I would favor a fixed stipend that stays with the job and not the person. (See §11.)

In my own experience (as an external candidate) I took a direct approach. In both cases where I was offered a headship I was prepared to divulge my present salary and fringe benefit package and let the dean make his best offer. But I wasn't asked for this information. In both cases good financial offers were made, and not much additional effort was needed to get what I thought appropriate.

If you are an external candidate, before going to the interview get: copies of the CVs of the faculty, a copy of the most recent external review or self-study of the department, catalogues for the graduate and undergraduate programs, the mission statement for the department and the college. Study them. I don't know that you have to memorize a lot. I didn't. But it helped to see what the departments and universities thought about themselves. You can also learn about the faculty and, after you spend a day talking to more people than you could ever remember, the vitae will help you begin putting names to faces. (Ah! That's the name of the guy that works in PDEs and went to Wabash College.)

Before going to the campus try to find out why they are going outside for a head. Perhaps, if this is possible, you can have an informal conversation with a friend there to discover some information that might not surface in any formal undertaking. Are there warring factions and no one can agree on an internal candidate? Are you being recruited to referee a bloody war? To stop one? It may just be that they regard recruiting an outside head as an opportunity to bring a fresh approach to the life of the department or to recruit an additional person with good research credentials. But you better figure out why and decide if you are up to their expectations. I don't think I would like to come from the outside to act as a referee. You are bound to get bloodied in the conflict, and there are more important things in life.

What are they looking for? A god? A czar? A figurehead? A researcher? How is the Mathematics Department regarded? A strong research department? A service department? Better to find out before you have to confront an offer.

How to impress the interviewing dean.

There may be some cynical interpretations of the title of this subsection. However, I am not implying that you should give any false impressions. As I have said before, the head and the dean will have many contacts, and any hint that you have not been sincere will have a negative effect. So you have to be honest and open; in other words, be yourself.

This all assumes you want the job, that nothing you have learned about the department has discouraged or soured you on the prospect of heading this department. What are some issues that you might address that will convey your priorities and make it likely you will get the appointment?

This is one place where it makes a great difference whether you are an internal or external candidate. As an external candidate you are unlikely to come for the interview, listen to the department's difficulties, and arrive at a remedy. If you do have ideas, express them. But try to avoid being too dramatic. Whatever solutions you think you have found are unlikely to stand very close scrutiny. In any case, the realities will be more vivid when you actually take over the job, and whatever preconceived plans you concoct are likely to be altered in the day-to-day operations.

One good approach might be to ask questions. (Always a good thing to do when you don't know the answers.) What is the dean's perception of the Mathematics Department? Does (s)he understand that mathematics has a life of its own, or does (s)he believe the department's main focus should be to service the rest of the university? What is the dean's greatest gripe about the Mathematics Department? Does (s)he feel that the university has struck a good balance between research and teaching?

How is the quality of teaching in the Mathematics Department? You'll undoubtedly get some negative comments here, so be prepared. Mathematics departments teach a large number of students who have been coerced into taking its courses. With few exceptions this results in a campus-wide feeling that the mathematics department is not a good teaching department. In fact, every mathematics department at a large state university that I am acquainted with has this reputation. This would be a good place to get in some of your personal philosophy about teaching, some experience with innovative teaching methods, or some accomplishments in teaching.

How familiar is the dean with calculus reform? Does (s)he feel that the department has been doing enough integrating of computer technology into its teaching? Does (s)he have an opinion about large classes in precalculus? Large classes in general?

Well, you get the idea. Try to understand the dean's perspective. If you get the job, you will be working with him/her. Later (§5) I'll talk about the agenda you should have and the importance of aligning that agenda with the dean's. It would be best to know that you can work with this dean now. The interview with the dean during a campus visit is the only opportunity you will have to get to know him/her before you take the job. You can talk to faculty members and get their impression. But I'll warn you that faculty have a different perception of what the dean does. They don't work with him/her, and they tend to focus on the bad news they hear or see. Besides, do you really want to decide whether to accept a job and change your life on hearsay evidence about the character and policies of the dean?

§3. Should you accept the appointment?

OK, it's an increase in salary — that's good. But you will have to work for that money. Your life is going to change. There is a great deal of independence that goes with the job of faculty member, and this is one of the things we all love about the profession. Becoming a head will mean that you will lose a lot of that independence and freedom (but not all of it). So accepting the job as chair should carry some rewards beyond the extra money. Believe me, the money alone is not enough. So here are some reasons for taking the job and some things to think about before you take it.

I have a dream.

Be careful. If your dream is not fully realized, what will happen? Will you feel like a failure? It is almost certain that your preconceived plans will not be completely brought to fruition. If this dream is essentially realized, what will you do then? You probably shouldn't take on the job if there is just one goal you want to reach.

Some of the preceding comments are probably irrelevant for those who have a fixed non-renewable term. Actually, the popular three-year term is, in my experience, too short to realize any dream. A three year term is essentially a guarantee for maintenance of the status quo. Perhaps, on a subconscious level, that is the reason for its existence.

I like people, and I like dealing with their problems.

A good reason; it usually persists. But don't expect your clients and the beneficiaries of your help to continue liking you. You will have to make decisions; some of them will be difficult, and some decisions will hurt and disappoint a subset of your faculty. Even when you give out a plum (a sabbatical, a reduced teaching load, travel funds), there may be others who will be jealous or think you made a mistake. Over time it can be hoped that most faculty will benefit from your headship and see the wisdom of having you as head and the justice and fairness of your actions. But expect to have some faculty upset with you over various time periods, and be certain there will be other faculty who will regret the day you became head. That's life and that's the job. (You might take some comfort in that they probably dislike you for who you are, not for the position you occupy.)

The cycle has come around, and it is my turn.

Some departments are like this. You are a good citizen and can do a good job, so go ahead and take your turn. But please have an agenda. If you don't, you will just be minding the store and hoping that no catastrophes occur. It really won't help the department. (On the other hand, maybe the department is just finishing one of those periods of internecine struggle that seem to happen occasionally, and a quiet interlude might just be what is best.) If the term is short and you cannot succeed yourself, keep the agenda short and simple. Make arrangements with your successor for you to stick with your project after your term expires so that it doesn't become one more unfulfilled departmental hope.

I've known heads in departments with rotating chairs who actually campaigned for the job and then just minded the store for three years. What a waste! Only that one individual benefitted — from an increase in salary and access to additional administrative jobs where they had a similarly undistinguished record. The department got nothing from the experience except an additional faculty member for whom there is diminished respect.

If I don't take it, someone worse will.

Actually, this is a pretty good reason, if it's true. This probably indicates, however, that something is wrong in the department. If all you do is play keep-away, you really won't do anyone a service. So confront the split that is implied by such a statement. If you really want to earn your colleagues' respect, set as your goal the spackling of this crack. It will be a more important accomplishment than increasing salaries. So be magnanimous, spread salve, heal wounds. Make your competitor the first recipient of your largesse.

§4. Why do I enjoy being a head?

Why do I enjoy ice cream? Brahms? Champagne? Actually, those questions are a bit easier to answer. Maybe a closer question to the one raised in the heading is why do I enjoy learning about subnormal operators? Questions about the pleasures of ice cream, Brahms, and champagne are questions of taste and pleasure. The questions about the joy of subnormal operators or being a head certainly also involve taste and pleasure, but the answers lie somewhat deeper.

After I had been a head for about a year and I would encounter friends at meetings and conferences, the question inevitably arose about my new job. I invariably answered, "I know I am not supposed to say this, but I enjoy the job." The last half of this response was true enough: I do enjoy being a head. The first part of that response is part of a reaction of mine to what I consider an element of intellectual dishonesty and/or a lack of intellectual perspicacity among many of our colleagues.

I have too often heard people complain about what a chore it is to do administrative jobs but simultaneously campaign for a headship. Well, I have never met anyone who was truly forced to become a head or a dean. In fact, it is my understanding that slavery was abolished long ago. I have met people who have become heads out of a sense of duty and who would rather have been left alone to do their research and teaching. Nevertheless, the notion persists that no one becomes a head unless they are forced or bribed to do the job. Mathematicians fail to realize that not everyone thinks the way they do at this particular time of their life. The pressure for conformity on this issue would make a religious zealot envious.

Maybe there is still part of the rebellious teenager in me, because I sometimes take a certain perverse joy in saying the unexpected, especially if I believe my audience has an ill-founded belief. So I openly profess certain beliefs and feelings in the full confidence that I am not the only person who believes or feels that way, regardless of how widely the contrary is proclaimed. So I state openly and publicly: Though I have frequently been moved by music, I have never been moved by a painting, and I do not enjoy art galleries; I do not enjoy playing chess; I like to play with my model railroad; I like big, shiny new cars; I enjoy being the head of a mathematics department.

It strikes me as strange that members of a profession that 98% of the population believes to be weird have difficulty understanding that not everyone in it feels the same way about its various aspects. Well, that's one of the mysteries that makes life interesting and perplexing, if sometimes irritating. But now that I have professed my right to my opinion and feelings about my job, I still have not said why I enjoy it.

First, I find people interesting. Human beings are incredibly complex and varied, and being a head allows me to see aspects I don't think I would have been exposed to as a professor. Sometimes the revelations are not a joy, but I still find this part of my education pleasant and interesting. Strangely enough, one of the people I have found to study and analyze is myself. I see myself reacting to new situations, new people, new problems, and I enjoy studying my reactions. I'll also tell you that my wife says I am a more understanding person since I came to Tennessee and that I am more attuned to personal relationships. Whether that is due to the job, a different approach to life resulting from getting older, or the very fact that we moved and changed so much of our lives, I cannot say.

I see the job of head as a succession of problems, and I enjoy trying to solve them. The problems are not the same as in the discipline; they call for different types of solutions. The problems are seldom well-posed, and the solutions are almost never unique. In attacking these problems, you must use a variety of tools, only one of which is logic and reason.

I like the challenge of setting a mathematical policy and trying to lead the department in that direction. I have always had a vision of mathematics and how this business should proceed, though that vision has not been the same throughout my career. I like articulating my vision and persuading my colleagues to pursue my dreams. That's what I call leadership. One of the joys of leadership is getting your organization to perform the way you think it should. Perhaps that is too abstract, but, as you read other sections in this book, it should become more concrete.

A very strong part of my vision for a mathematics department is the way I think faculty should be treated. Too often our profession has been abused, often by its own members. From making teaching assignments to supporting research, to making available appropriate supplies and secretarial help, to promoting ambitions of the virtuous, a head can enhance the professional life of the faculty. With a rare exception or two, such acts are appreciated and contribute to the development of the field. It is a worthy undertaking.

When I was a faculty member, I did not feel my influence extended far beyond my classroom. In many ways I had reason to feel otherwise, maybe more so than most mathematicians. I had 16 PhD students and wrote successful textbooks. So, rationally, I know my presence was felt. But by being a head, especially one at a large state university, I believe I affect mathematics education on a very broad front, even if many of those affected are not conscious of my role. But when I realize some good things I have done and how many I have affected, there is a reward.

Finally there is what may seem a bit too idealistic and romantic a reason. I have had a good life as a mathematician. I think that one of the real keys to happiness is finding something you truly enjoy doing and convincing someone to pay you to do it. Being a professor of mathematics has enabled me to do that. Being a head allows me the opportunity of making a contribution in kind to the profession.

Setting the Stage

§5. The agenda.

Every head should have an agenda: a collection of goals, priorities, and ambitions for the department. Many heads do not. I am not going to deride the heads that do not, but exhort them to get one. For the department heads who have been around for awhile and don't have the energy or enthusiasm for change and improvement, maybe you ought to consider stepping down and turning over control of the department to someone who does. I know this may seem harsh and self-righteous, but if you have some loyalty to the department and the institution, this may be the most loving thing you can do. The professional lives of your faculty and the academic lives of your students are at stake. If the faculty are all satisfied with the *status quo*, maybe you should take a close look to be sure that this is not the result of complacency. This business is too serious to deprive them of leadership and subject them to stasis.

The role of a head is to lead. You cannot lead without a goal.

I understand that some colleges and universities are just trying to keep their head above water, coping daily with the chores of academic survival. That is a sad state of affairs. But every institution has to define itself and try to offer something that makes it a desirable place to go to school. Every college needs a vision of itself and its future. The same applies to departments.

Whether it is a community college, a large state university, or a choice liberal arts college, there should be a reason that students will choose to go to this place for their education rather than elsewhere. In the case of the community college and some state universities, this reason is often the convenience of the location and the low tuition. Too often the administrators of such places believe this to be enough; these are sad places to work, and it is manifest in the morale of the faculty. How much better to have something that they do better than most institutions: a liberal arts program with an exceptionally heavy emphasis on writing; a specialty in producing some of the best high

15

school mathematics teachers in a three-state area; a nursing program that successfully places all its graduates; an exceptional bachelors degree in Islamic studies, or Japanese studies, or Afro-American studies, or women's studies. With the enormous pool of talent that resides in the academic world, it would not take much additional effort on the part of anyone who runs a campus to carve out an area of uniqueness and quality. This would boost the morale not only of the faculty directly involved in the area of uniqueness, but across the campus; everyone would feel they were working at a special place and it would show.

If your dean is not a good one, I can't give you any advice, save to see if you can get rid of him/her. That may not be easy but it may be the appropriate agenda. This is a sticky business, fraught with peril. Be aware that even if you succeed, you may pay a price. Other deans and administrators often cast a leery eye at someone who has attacked a member of the club.

It is the agenda that will give your term of office definition and direction. Leadership means setting and enunciating a vision. If you lose sight of where you are going, you will never get there.

A good dean or president will want to preside over a quality institution. Give them that opportunity. Know the dean's agenda and the process (s)he uses for making budget decisions. You should try to fit your agenda and crusades for resources into that framework. Remember that if you launch a program or initiate a reform that is successful, it will reflect well on the dean as well as on you. They want success just as you do. If you really can't do this for philosophical or personality reasons, you might want to reconsider taking the job. Otherwise you will either be forced to put all your plans on hold and just become a caretaker, or perhaps you will so antagonize the dean that his/her ire will be transferred to the department, causing it to suffer.

Suppose there are topics and programs that are important to you and your department but the dean has no ideas, opinions, or plans that are connected with this part of your agenda. What to do? Actually, this can be one of the most desirable of situations. Begin to educate your dean why this is so important. Make sure (s)he sees the wisdom and necessity of your agenda and that if your plan is brought to fruition, there will be glory for the college as well as for the department. The difficult part of this situation is that with limited resources the dean may have other parts of his/her agenda that will compete for funds with your project, and this will put you lower on the list of priorities.

§6. Some ideas for an agenda.

I am not so arrogant as to suggest what you should do with your term as head. It is up to you and depends more on local conditions than any abstract concepts of how departments should function. But here are a few ideas for inclusion in an agenda. If you will, these are ideas for projects. Actually, this is a list of some of the things that I have been doing since becoming head, and I offer them more to stimulate thought than as a blueprint for conducting your term of office.

Improving teaching.

My experience is that teaching in most mathematics departments is rather good. This flies in the face of the popular culture. Complaints about mathematics teaching seem endemic in academia. I am not totally sure why this is, but I strongly believe it has a lot to do with the fact that we teach large numbers of students who are being forced to take our courses and would rather be elsewhere. Studying mathematics is also somewhat like studying a foreign language. You have to work at it steadily, day in, day out. You can't forget about it for a week and get caught up with an intense weekend of reading. So we start each semester, when we teach a freshman-level course, with a semi-hostile audience. Before the semester ends a high percentage of the students have not succeeded as they would have liked, and the teacher is the natural recipient of their ire.

As I walk the halls and overhear what is going on in the classrooms, my impression is that what is going on is good. People give conscientious and clear explanations, and they convey an interest and, sometimes, an enthusiasm for what they are teaching. At the higher levels, the enthusiasm is palpable. I have seen mathematicians pour themselves into courses, recapturing the excitement they experienced while a student.

I know there are louts out there, and I have met the dregs of the profession; I met them as a student and as a professor and as a head. But they're rare. More rare than the shining lights. The vast majority of college mathematics teachers are knowledgeable, articulate, and accessible to the students.

So if I think the teaching of mathematics is so good, why am I suggesting improving it for your agenda? First, it can always be improved. Second, it is vital for the health of your department that the faculty and graduate students think about teaching and discuss it. This is often done in an informal way, talking about classes at lunch or a departmental party.

I remember talking at a party with a colleague of mine about how teaching polynomial calculus and finite mathematics seemed to be the dominant topic of conversation. Weren't there better topics: leaking roofs, wet crawl spaces, presidential politics, Fermat's Last Theorem, subnormal operators? (But, please, spare me the conversation about little league soccer.) Most of those classes were taught in sections of 250 students, and what I think was going on, but didn't realize at the time, was group therapy.

One semester I organized what I called a teaching seminar. It met only three times that semester. I bought all of the GTA's a copy of Steven Krantz's book, *How to Teach Mathematics*. At the three meetings, a panel of four faculty members, including myself, discussed a series of 16 topics addressed in Krantz's book. There was lively discussion by the audience — I declared the event a success. Attendance, while not universal, was good. I think it is important for GTA's and perspective mathematicians to understand that there are functioning mathematicians for whom teaching is an important activity and one that commands time, effort, and respect.

Improving research.

This is a lot harder to do. Everyone is aware that you can't just tell people to start doing better research without being laughed at. There are a wide variety of factors that motivate mathematicians to do research, but I suspect no one is motivated by a dictum from the head.

About the only way a head can improve research at his/her department is by recruiting well. On the other hand, you can make conditions that support research improve: better perks for the productive, more travel funds, a bigger colloquium budget. All this will improve morale amongst the researchers and scholars, and your colleagues will sense your commitment. This might not increase the absolute value of the research being done in your department, but it will increase the contribution of that research toward the quality of the local scholarly life.

Review the PhD prelims.

This is an exercise that all graduate departments go through periodically. It is hard work, generates heat, but is essential for intellectual health. The department should see what others are doing and ask whether the degree requirements are appropriate for the faculty of today. New faculty are recruited and old faculty retire or migrate. With these transmogrifications, areas of emphasis in the department are altered.

Revise the undergraduate major program.

This is done less frequently than reviewing PhD preliminary examinations. What undergraduates should study and learn is fairly standard. We undertook such a revision recently. When the University of Tennessee changed from quarters to semesters, it went through a whole series of curriculum changes. These were in effect for many years, and it was decided that the new requirements were not meeting the department's aims. So the Undergraduate Committee devoted about a year and a half to making changes.

Contact alumni.

A place where almost every large mathematics department falls down is keeping in touch with its alumni. Alumni can be helpful. We'd like them to contribute to the department, but they are also a good source of information for the current students. What kind of careers do they have? What is the value of the degree? Alumni can also be a source of feedback for the faculty on the effectiveness of the program.

Smaller colleges seem to have a better record in this area. They have a better sense of the importance of the alumni. Maybe because smaller colleges tend to be private and more dependent on alumni for their existence.

Improve relations with the area schools.

The elementary, middle, and high school teachers need your help. If you do it properly, they will be enormously appreciative, and you will get better-prepared students coming into your classes.

I am in the minority when it comes to assessing the quality of education being offered in our public schools. I am not talking about schools where crime is a problem; that's a question on which I have no expertise. But on the average, it may be that schools are doing a decent job, given their boundary conditions.

I know the results of comparisons between SAT scores and math tests given to students from different countries, and I have seen the students in my own calculus class and what they don't know. But what isn't so clear to me is whether these comparisons are being made in a legitimate way.

I do not know the figures, but we all know that a larger percentage of eighteen-year-olds are going to college today than 25 years ago. Therefore a larger percentage of them take the SAT than did 25 years ago. Unless you think that intelligence is evenly distributed across the population, the average score has to decrease under these circumstances.

To put it another way, with some exaggeration and simplification for illustration, let's assume that in any given year the students who try to go to college are roughly the smartest students getting out of school. If one year 10% of high schoolers go to college and another year 20% go, it stands to reason that the average intelligence of the college-bound populations has significantly decreased.

The calculus class I taught two years ago was not as well prepared as the one I taught 25 years ago. (There is always the possibility that such a statement is a result of seeing the past in a golden glow, but I don't think so in this case.) But not only has the percentage of high schoolers who go to college increased in 25 years, the percentage of college students who take calculus has also increased. Is it any wonder that the average mathematical ability of calculus students has decreased?

The educational system in the United States is unique in the world. Every other country has designed its system to filter out a very large number of students and prevent them from making it to college. (Many, however, have a technical school system we should envy.) We are dedicated to maximizing the amount of time every student spends in school. So when I see a study comparing average test scores of high school seniors in the US with another country or some group of countries, I feel as though I am watching either stupidity or malevolence on parade. This is a comparison between non-corresponding population samples.

Actually, there is a large collection of people who have a fiduciary interest in criticizing public education. Problems take money to fix and are the fault of the opposition.

But with all this, the teachers are under a lot of pressure and need support. You devote considerable time staying mathematically

vibrant. School teachers barely have time to catch their breath between classes and paper grading. They could use a little help master-
ing a computer and integrating it into their algebra course. Having
them reconnect with some of the excitment that attracted them to
mathematics in the first place might also be an aid.

§7. Clean house or resurrect?

Actually, the title of this section is something of a myth. At the
very least it is what might be termed an academic legend. Back
in the good old days, when men were men and giants walked the earth,
there were incidents where a department head would be brought in
from the outside and told to rebuild the mathematics department.
Note the word here is "rebuild," not create. One of the first duties
of this new head, so the legend goes, was to get rid of non-productive
faculty and replace them by sterling researchers. The new head had
the prerogative to inform select older faculty that they could expect
to never get a raise again and to teach twice as much as before.
What happened to these faculty members was never made clear to
me. Maybe they accepted their fate (not graciously, I hope and pre-
sume) or maybe they changed jobs.

I believe this happened, but before 1965. The reason I think
such scenes were played out is that the story has been told me by reliable people; the reason I say it happened before 1965 is that's when
I got my PhD and I know of no such incident during my academic
lifetime. (I do know of such an incident in recent years in computer
science. That corner of academia is at the evolutionary stage mathematics was about 30 years ago, when disgruntled faculty had a place
to move. Given that the laws that govern behavior in the academic
world transcend disciplines, this probably means that the legend of
the department head who is given the right to be a czar-cossack is
true.)

Strangely enough, many mathematicians seem to regard such
tales with glee. Maybe visions of a few of their colleagues who would
certainly bite the dust under such a regime brings them such joy that
their judgment is temporarily clouded. In any case, the facts of the
present day relegate such scenes to the realm of fantasy.

For one thing, mathematicians cannot move to another job as
they used to. A professor who is really irritated can make a head's
job a living nightmare. The head can freeze the professor's salary, but

the professor can be a lousy teacher, disrupt faculty meetings, spread cynicism amongst the graduate students, etc. It is much easier to be creative in seeking revenge than in doing research or being a creative teacher.

But most departments have missions that encompass a variety of jobs besides teaching and research. All state universities and many private ones are interested in working with local schools. The Putnam team needs a coach. The computer network needs an intelligent, dedicated person to oversee it. Incorporating computers into good mathematics teaching is an important and difficult task that researchers often do not take on. What is happening with the honors program? Do you need an associate head?

One of the main tasks of a department head is to offer every colleague the opportunity for a satisfying professional life. (See §8.) People who have a PhD tend to be intelligent. People stop doing research for any number of reasons, but seldom because they have gone brain dead. It is possible to lose interest in proving theorems but retain a love and appreciation of the subject; to still feel a desire to be creative, but without the long hours of frustration and isolation needed to do research. I have told friends that one of the joys I get from writing books is the near linear relation between the time I spend writing and what I have to show for it. Two hours of working on a book usually produces twice as much as one hour. The function that expresses research results as dependent on time is constant almost everywhere with occasional sharp jump discontinuities.

At this point the reader is probably saying something like, "You have never met my colleague Zatsfrats. He *is* brain dead. He *is* procrastination personified and has turned sloth into a full-time pursuit." Actually I have met Zatsfrats. Fortunately, not too often. There are milder variations on Zatsfrats: colleagues who will never expand into other activities. They seem to relish the easy life of teaching a couple of courses and spending the remainder of their time at the golf course, the tennis court, or just bothering any student or colleague they can buttonhole in the hall or common room.

Well I believe that teaching two courses a semester is not a full-time job. So if a professor is not doing research and is not involved in any other activities that contribute to the teaching and service mission of the department, (s)he should teach more courses. I've required such faculty to teach extra courses. They objected, I insisted, and it was done. It was neither the proudest nor the most distasteful part of the job. It was just one of the job's obligations.

On the other hand, it is erroneous to think of teaching an extra course as a punitive action. As careers progress it is normal for research productivity to decline. Teaching is an honorable activity, and I cannot be persuaded that asking someone to teach a third or fourth course is punitive.

Understand, however, the psychology of being asked or required to declare that your status has changed. Our academic culture has attached a great deal of prestige to research and a two-course teaching load. Altering this, perhaps, changes the label of the faculty member in the eyes of his colleagues. But teaching is part of our professional activity. Each faculty member should play a productive role in the department's life; and if the research and service aren't there, teaching is a worthy alternative.

There is, of course, an ironical twist in this scheme. Too often the faculty who have dropped out of research and have no desire or inclination to become involved in other aspects of academic life are people you would prefer not to have teaching more. These are the people that politicians and critics of academia love to expose and write about. They are the walking, breathing arguments against tenure. If I had such a situation, I'd ask the faculty member to teach more but try to work on improving his/her teaching. I don't say this can be done. But often teaching that has deteriorated is a result of a change in attitude. Why has this happened? If you can answer that, you might rescue a colleague.

The final wrinkle in all this is salary. I'll say more about this in §11 below, but it should be understood that you cannot ask someone to redirect their career and not reward them for it. If a colleague no longer does research but actively pursues the integration of computers into instruction, his/her raises have to be determined on the basis of this work. This colleague must be rewarded for success.

§8. Offering a quality professional life.

One of the main duties of a head is to provide the faculty with the opportunity for a professional life of quality. If you do this, you will reap many rewards and many of your sins will be forgiven. Your faculty will appreciate and benefit from such efforts, and the students will benefit from being taught by people who feel respected and valued and satisfied. I think this is one of the two or three most important functions of the head.

Of course the title of this section is generic and requires specificity. Part of increasing the quality of the professional life involves recruiting and getting raises and other financial support for the faculty. These are the big issues and are covered by their own sections in this book. But there are numerous small things you can and should do to improve academic life. I am not going to attempt to list all of these. I'll only mention a few, especially some that might not be universally regarded as contributing to the quality of the *professional* life.

Be sure the secretarial staff is courteous; don't allow the faculty to be discourteous to the staff. Some old adages are true. Courtesy is contagious. Creating a professional atmosphere is a lot easier when you don't have to contend with a breakdown in basic human relations.

Respect is a crucial ingredient to any enterprise that involves several people. An essential part of the nature of respect is that it must be reciprocated. It is a statistically demonstrable fact that secretaries have more respect for faculty than conversely. One group whose professional life the head must cultivate and improve is the secretarial staff; this will result in an improvement of the faculty's life. See §16.

Make sure that paper, Xeroxing, and phones are adequate. Mathematics departments live on paper for exams, researching, scratching. If the supply is meager, you will hear about it. In my second year as head the department faced a tight budget. I reacted by limiting photocopying, especially of exams. I figured we could let the students furnish blue books or their own writing paper, so I suggested that exams be duplicated with no room for the students to write out their solutions. One of the worst things I ever did. The complaints far exceeded the value of any savings. Almost no one complained about the lack of travel funds, but everyone complained about the inconvenience, the greater likelihood of cheating, the increased time needed for grading and processing exams administered in this way. When I found I had a bit more money half way through the year, this was the first money saver I abandoned.

Try to get the best computing equipment possible and good technical assistance. If faculty do not have access to the latest computing equipment, don't expect them to do good work integrating technology with teaching. For faculty who use computers in their research, this has added urgency and creates a new set of issues for mathematicians that our friends in the physical sciences have been struggling with forever.

Fight for travel money for faculty and students. A lot of people outside academic life regard faculty travel as a perk. In fact, travel for many in business is a perk. A salesman traveling to see clients is recognized as an activity that results in sales and therefore income. Travel to a golf resort for a seminar on the latest techniques in real estate development, where classes meet only in the morning and no one ever takes attendance, are suspected of being a tax deductible fringe benefit. So travel by faculty to go to research conferences at nice places is suspect for the public. In fact, it is an essential part of our profession, whether the travel involves research or teaching.

Let the faculty teach courses outside their specialty if they wish. This is a good form of development. Anyone can get stale teaching the same thing year in and year out, even if it is in their specialty. Letting an analyst teach algebra can reinvigorate the juices and perhaps increase the enthusiasm in the classroom.

Make sure the seminars run smoothly; put out weekly calendars with the seminar schedule and anything else that might be of interest to the faculty. Not many faculty will go to a seminar they are not closely connected to, but they like hearing what is going on. The same is true for students.

§9. Departmental personalities.

Each department has a personality. Some departments are rather neutral, but I tend to regard "neutral" as a personality. Most departments are, however, anything but neutral, and often the departmental complexion is a reflection of the head's personality and his/her approach to the job of administration. To paraphrase Tolstoy, happy departments are all happy for the same reason. Unhappy departments are unhappy for different reasons. Ultimately, the unhappiness or happiness in a department starts with the head.

The two departments I am most familiar with have markedly contrasted personalities. Others I have visited either as a colloquium speaker, short-term visitor, or reviewer have characters still different from these two. Others I experienced as a student are also different, but the observations of a student are notoriously unreliable. (This is not a criticism of students; it also applies to me when I inhabited that state of being. Students bring such dramatically different perspectives — idealistic, persecuted, disappointed — that their opinions about departments tend to be inconsistent and far more influenced by other students and their current difficulties.)

Why do these different departmental characteristics exist? One ingredient, a most important one, is the variety of personalities in the faculty. But the type of people who join a department is influenced by a variety of factors such as the degree of focus of the department on teaching and research, geography, the urbanity of the campus's location, and, very often, the personality of the head.

The Courant Institute at New York University is significantly influenced by its location in the heart of Greenwich Village. Many faculty are in their office for just a portion of a couple of days a week. Graduate classes meet once a week for two hours, often starting late in the afternoon or early evening. Part of the reason for this is to afford graduate classes to students who are working full time, but a large reason for this unusual schedule is to minimize commuting time for the faculty.

Contrast this with Indiana University, set in a small town, where many faculty members come to work on foot or by bike. Just about all the faculty there are on campus all day, every weekday; some even return in the evening and on the weekend.

Since this is a book on being a head, let's ask how the personality of the head can influence the department's personality? I remember going to one department to give a colloquium. After meeting my host and talking mathematics, we went to meet the head for lunch. Almost immediately after the hellos, this head began complaining to me about the size of the department's phone bill. This ridiculous, boring conversation continued well after getting my sandwich. Would you be surprised if I told you this department tended to the morose?

If you are a pessimist, it's likely that the department will not feel cheery about its long-range prospects. If you are seldom in your office, don't be surprised if you have trouble finding a colleague. If you tend to be late for meetings and appointments, expect to be kept waiting on occasion.

I know a former head who initiated new faculty to the department with a lousy teaching schedule. Typically such new colleagues would get one class at 8:00 in the morning and another at 5:00 or 6:00 in the afternoon at this urban campus. I was told he did this for the first semester or two to let everyone know who was boss. Was this guy an abused child? I think my reaction would have been to start looking for another job. Certainly I could never forget such treatment. No one doubts that a head, certainly one with a long term, has authority. Such a capricious and blatant exhibition of power probably tends to diminish the head's prerogative rather than enhance it. Authority, like respect, is one of those attributes that decreases when you loudly proclaim your right to it.

§10. Ethics.

My first piece of advice on ethics is that you should have some. If you don't, take up another profession. I am going to assume that no one gets to be a department head who is a sociopath, even though I have heard about heads who cling to the edge of this category.

Becoming a head seems to accentuate certain personality traits. Mean people get meaner. Manipulators encounter their ideal environment. Plotters have little difficulty finding co-conspirators. On the other hand, certain good personality traits have to be modified and subdued. We sweet people have to harden a bit; you just cannot keep everyone happy all the time. Since taking advantage of a head offers a bigger payoff, more people will be tempted to try. So the trusting had better develop a bit of skepticism. But ethics should transcend personality.

There may be times when you are tempted to lie. Who isn't? As head there are unpleasant situations that can be avoided (temporarily) by telling a lie. Be aware, though, that the consequences of lying for a head are far more onerous than for other faculty.

Sometimes not telling the whole truth is not necessarily lying. Certainly you don't have to divulge every piece of information you have. You also have a right to refuse to answer some questions. But if someone asks you a question they have no right to ask, do you have an obligation to tell the truth? If answering "No comment" would convey information to someone and they don't have a right to that information, are you lying if you don't tell the truth? I (and you) associate something immoral with the term lying, but I am not convinced that every statement is either a lie or a truth.

While an editor for the *Proceedings of the American Mathematical Society*, I was asked by an author who had a paper rejected, "The referee was Jack Blitchinrass, wasn't it?" In fact, Jack was the referee. But I answered, "No. He is too young for me to use as a referee of your paper." I did not hesitate to say this because the author had no right to ask that question. If I had said "No comment," I think he would have surmised the truth. As it was, he was thrown off track by my reply, and I succeeded in maintaining the anonymity of the referee — a worthy goal. I see nothing immoral in what I did.

Situations like the one I just described irritate me. Another approach might have been to look the author in the eye and say, "I can't believe you asked me that. You know it's not professional to ask such a question." Maybe next time.

When I am asked an appropriate question, I answer truthfully. I have too many dealings with too many people to do otherwise; my memory banks are insufficient to retain any intricate web of deception. I also make it a habit of being forthright and direct in my dealings. This is a form of honesty that some, apparently, feel is not the best policy. On occasion I have crossed the line of demarcation between 'frank' and 'blunt'. Sometimes I cross that line on purpose. If someone is not doing a good job, I believe in telling them so. It's better that they should know what they are facing than be hit with an unexpected catastrophe.

A good code of personal ethics is essential for a head. It is important that others know they can trust and rely on you and that you set a high standard for the staff and your colleagues. This is another way you can influence the departmental personality (§9).

If anything ever appears slightly questionable, the head should stop, think, and consider whether there is an ethical problem. I discuss such questions a lot with my wife. I find her non-academic view enlightening. Academics are often too close to problems to recognize them. I also have given strict instructions to my staff that no one, including me, has the right to ask them to do anything that violates their personal code. If they ever feel that I have asked them to violate their ethics, they have an obligation to let me know. I assure them that such an occurrence will be because of my obtuseness. (Actually, they are so straight I probably don't have to do this.)

You and your staff will deal with money, and where there is money there is the possibility of misbehavior. Most departments have a petty cash fund. Unless you have safeguards, this is an irresistible temptation to many people who will have access to it. Certainly the head should never abuse it. Put exactly one person in charge and demand accountability.

In the name of speed and expediency you will, perhaps, tread close to the unethical. Your staff might also feel this and wonder whether you are pushing them to act against their code or merely being too hasty. So make them clearly understand where you stand. You don't want to wake one morning and read the newspaper's exposé of budget irregularities in the mathematics department. Also you will acquire enemies, and you should take precautions lest you unwittingly furnish them information that, at the least, will embarrass you.

The point here is that the crush of daily business may lead you to quick solutions that introduce ethical difficulties. As innocent as your intentions may be, you want to avoid having anyone think you operate unethically. Put some ethical speed bumps in your path.

Another potential source of ethical conflict is in the administration of grants. I still regard a grant as the property of the principal investigator (PI). Before I became head, my grants were too often tampered with and picked at, and this continues to have an influence on me. But such an attitude can lead to problems, especially with large grants that have money to hire students or temporary staff and give workshops. Occasionally PIs, regarding the grant as theirs, believe they have the right to do whatever they want as long as it furthers a good end. But spending money from a grant for something the grant was not awarded to support is illegal as well as unethical. Money from a grant obtained to conduct a teacher workshop cannot be used to pay a student to do a library search in subnormal operators. Even if the student is working in the area for which the grant was awarded, both the PI and the head must remember that this is a student. The work cannot be allowed to interfere with the student's studies.

While on the subject of grants, here is a point worth mentioning even though there is no ethical problem attached. When the department head signs a grant proposal, (s)he is agreeing to cover any cost overrun incurred by the PI while carrying out the project. Some grants can get very complicated, and careful administration of the grant is good preventive medicine for avoiding a budget mess.

The American Mathematical Society has a statement on ethics in the profession (http://www.ams.org/committee/profession/ethics. html) and another on ethics in employment (http://www.ams.org/ committee/profession/supportive-prgms.html). Read them and think about them. These documents frame a perspective of our current professional culture.

As I write this the job market for mathematicians in academia is depressed (and depressing). There are many ethical considerations connected with hiring, and, in times such as these, there is a strong temptation on the part of departments and universities to push the boundaries of the acceptable. Some departments have begun to offer one-year, non-renewable instructorships for new PhDs, often at reduced salaries. I regard this as unacceptable behavior. True, this gives someone a job. But it is exploiting the despondent market and the fears of the young.

Recently a young mathematician obtained a three-year, tenure-track job at a less-than-prestigious university. After a few months on the job he was informed that they had changed his status to a one-year visitor. Truly an abomination. That university is marked in my book. I wish there was a way to sanction such institutions. My friend shied away from litigation both because of the time and cost and because he (correctly) feared being tainted.

There are many other situations that might arise that will raise questions in ethics. I'll close with one more. It is related to the concept of nepotism. There was a time when nepotism was a clearly defined subject with simple rules governing it. No one can be the supervisor of a directly related person. This also abetted discrimination against women. But that is a topic in itself, one that will still probably generate heat.

At a recent meeting a fellow department head discussed a problem currently demanding his attention. The "significant other" (I personally prefer the term "mate") of one of his faculty was a job candidate for a position in his department. No problem there. But the colleague felt (s)he had a right to participate in the discussion about whether to hire the mate. While acknowledging the propriety in excluding a candidate's spouse from such discussions, this mathematician felt this to be a different situation and his/her presence a right they wanted to exercise.

My response was astonishment that there was any doubt that this mathematician should recuse himself/herself from the discussion and any subsequent vote. With the courts awarding palimony and other financial settlements to splitting mates, society has clearly decided that if two people cohabit they should be considered as married, with all the privileges and obligations. If they live like a married couple, and walk like a married couple, and quack like a married couple, they are a married couple. The conflict of interest is clear. Whether the job candidate is the spouse, brother, child, or mate of a colleague, the issue is the same. The presence of someone in a discussion about a candidate with whom that person is personally involved will diminish frankness and warp the expressed opinions. If this colleague cannot trust the head to maintain fairness in personnel matters, (s)he should seek employment elsewhere.

Personnel Matters

§11. Salaries.

There are several aspects to the topic of salaries. Some I'll only touch on here and cover in more depth in other sections (like §14 on recruiting). Other aspects, like raises, are treated in their own section (§12).

Whenever you contemplate questions about salaries, remember a fundamental fact about human nature. Interfering with a person's money will stir up more anger quicker than just about anything. The only other thing that produces as strong a reaction is messing with their children. Tread carefully.

Yours relative to the rest of the faculty's.

This is a tricky subject. It is fundamental that you must keep the respect and good will of your colleagues. One easy way to cause a rift is to have your salary way ahead of the pack and not render good service for the dollar. I believe that a high salary alone is not a cause for the rift, unless it is unduly gotten. Let's look at a couple of examples.

First there is Professor Axalot. He/she belongs to a department that has periodic elections for its head. Professor Axalot has just won the latest round of the administrative popularity contest and begins his/her negotiations with the dean. As part of that process Professor Axalot obtains a raise that moves him/her from the middle of the full professor range to near the top. This will quite likely raise a few eyebrows (at the least). It may cast a pall over Professor Axalot's term. This assumes that the faculty learn about it, but this is almost certain to happen. The point is that Professor Axalot has sent a message to his/her colleagues that (s)he has become head for personal gain and is really not putting the department first. Professors tend not to look with kindness on such actions, especially if the salaries in the department are low compared to national standards. If Professor Axalot manages to accomplish a lot during his/her term, then (s)he may be saved. Maybe! If not, (s)he will have a difficult time moving back to the faculty at the conclusion of their term and probably should consider moving higher up the administrative chain (or lower, depending on your degree of cynicism). This of course will deepen the resentment of the faculty and make it even more difficult for Professor Axalot to return to the life of a professor.

Professor Bestbook is in a department with a similar process for choosing its head. But Professor Bestbook's salary is at the low end of the full professors. A significant raise comes when (s)he takes office, putting him/her in the upper middle of the salary range. In addition (s)he also obtains an extra $4000 for the colloquium fund and two additional Teaching Assistantships. Here the coffee room conversation is likely to go something like this. Well, Bestbook really was underpaid. Frankly I would never have done the job if my salary had been that low; I probably wouldn't have even stood for election. If Bestbook continues to do for us as (s)he already has, the department has got its money's worth.

Professor Clampdown is recruited from another university especially to be the head. The salary (s)he gets puts him/her at the top of the scale. Clampdown is in a position that has some pressure. Even without salary consideration, Professor Clampdown has pressure. (See §2, "Interviewing for the job.") The high salary indicates a vote of high confidence by the department since it is undoubtedly true that the dean discussed the salary with some group of faculty. But be aware that confidence implies expectations. If you want to experience a truly ugly situation, let Professor Clampdown fail to live up to expectations. If (s)he fails to deliver the kind of optimistic view of the future that his/her interview generated and that resulted in a salary out of line with the rest of the faculty, Professor Clampdown will have great difficulty remaining on this faculty after being forced to resign the headship. Hopefully the salary is sufficiently large that with minimum raises (s)he can coast until retirement.

The point of this issue is that as soon as heads set themselves apart from their colleagues, whether it be in salary, unusual perks, or anything that is not "usual and ordinary", there had better be a good reason for it and the head's later actions had better justify this distinction. Faculty in their collective wisdom (and in this case the wisdom is correct) understand that as soon as heads begin to set themselves apart, there is trouble around the bend. If you want to be a good head, to earn your colleagues respect, to have your name mentioned in the future with hallowed reverence and a longing for the good old days when heads were heads and giants walked the earth, understand your faculty and remain one with them. It's really what they are hoping for when they chose you.

How to compare salaries.

Most full professors earn more than most assistant professors. So how do you compare their salaries? Well, maybe you aren't interested in comparing such extremes. How do you compare any two professors' salaries? OK, the number system is well ordered. But does the fact that Professor Q has had a PhD ten years longer than Professor J have a bearing?

Another application of spreadsheets to departmental administration that I find useful is to subtract a fixed amount from each faculty member's salary. (I just do this in the spreadsheet, not in real life.) This fixed amount is roughly the salary of a fresh PhD. Then I divide each difference by the number of years the faculty member has had the PhD.

It isn't perfect but this does provide me with a method of comparison. If this difference quotient for Professor Q is large relative to the rest of the faculty, it means Professor Q is being rewarded for his/her efforts. This method has a number of drawbacks. Choosing the amount to subtract, for instance, can radically alter the numbers, especially at the lower ranks.

By the way, like all things to do with salary, this kind of number crunching makes a certain type of faculty member very nervous. Each department has its share of lawyer wannabes who want to have it all tied down and neatly trimmed. I haven't figured whether they believe there is a perfect way to determine salaries or are just ornery.

Salaries to new hires and the equity problem.

Justice is a virtue and has a place when discussing salaries and raises. But another factor is the law of supply and demand. Your job as head is to improve the department. If you can do this and dispense justice at the same time, I take my hat off to you. You have earned your chair at the great institute in the sky. But it is quite possible that at some point you will have to offer a new hire more money than someone who is on your faculty and has been there for some time. Do it if the new hire will improve the department.

There is a sentiment in some academic circles that no one should be hired at a salary higher than that of the lowest-paid person in the department at the same rank. This kind of thinking comes from those who tend to view the university and its departments as a kind of club. Perhaps their careers have not turned out as they thought they would and they cannot figure out why. So let's just all stick together. We may be miserable, but at least we're together.

I try never to lose someone to another university because of money. This doesn't mean I pay extraordinarily high salaries. But I match the competition and my dean backs me. No one we have made an offer to has ever come with a truly larger salary offer from another university. The differences tend to be small. Most of my colleagues want to be in a department that is on the move (up) and back me when I offer whatever is needed to get a good new colleague. But some strongly disagree.

There is a department I am acquainted with that had a practice of trying to maintain equity with its new hires. It tended to pay salaries that were below the market rate. Occasionally they were able to hire a good mathematician. The policy never raised anyone's salary, made no one happy, and sowed the seeds for future discontent. It also gave the dean a distorted picture of salaries in the profession. A dean recognizes compression as insidious and will usually try to do something about it.

§12. Giving raises.

How do you decide who to give raises to and how much to give? This is a tough question and one for which there is no set answer. I do think that raises should be used to improve the department and the college/university. So here is the first principle that should govern a raise strategy.

The First Aim of a Raise: *The hard working, productive faculty should be rewarded and the sloths should be punished.*

If you do not think people respond to rewards, you are more of an idealist than I am. Sometimes the rewards people pursue have little to do with money — fame, popularity, immortality, approval, psychological fulfillment, for example. But money is a motivation for many, whether that money is desired for its absolute self or as a tangible measure of accomplishment. So resolve that your raise strategies will go toward motivating people to contribute to the improvement of the department.

No raise strategy is going to please everyone. To do this, the strategy you follow would not only have to give each of your colleagues what they think they deserve, but just as importantly (this is even the more important aspect for some poor souls) the differences in the raises amongst the faculty must fit the preconceived pattern of each individual faculty member. Professor Jones can be quite happy with his/her raise, but when (s)he discovers how much Professor Smith received, the head is thought to have a bizarre sense of judgment. Each member of the faculty carries around in the recess of his/her psyche a linear ordering (with some equivalence classes) of the quality of the faculty, and no two such orderings agree. So there will always be people who are upset with your raise decisions. Don't even try or pretend to try to achieve happiness with a raise strategy. The goal of the raise has to be something else. If you are fair and follow a few common sense rules, over the long haul you will succeed: the virtuous will be rewarded and the wicked punished.

Let's look at a few strategies for deciding on raises and their attendant virtues and drawbacks. First a couple of extreme cases.

(a) Across the board, equal percentages.

Actually, after a period in which there are no raises this has an appeal to it. In my own experience of no raises for two years, everyone had suffered an erosion in their buying power, so there was some sense in giving everyone a lift. This also has the virtue of being easy to administer. The drawbacks are serious. First, it violates the First Aim of a Raise; it fails to give the virtuous an indication that their virtues are appreciated. If Professor Bedrock's publishing three papers, having a PhD and a Masters student, coaching the Putnam team, and chairing the graduate committee resulted in the same reward as that given Professor Idleby, who taught 2 courses a semester, played golf, and tended a vegetable garden, Bedrock might justifiably wonder why (s)he is working so hard.

An equally valid criticism of the across-the-board raise with equal percentages is that it exacerbates the salary differences between junior and senior faculty. If Professor Newbright makes an average salary, give it an index of 100, and Professor Thigjig has a salary index of 160, a 5% raise makes their indicies 105 and 168, respectively. So the difference between their indices has gone from 60 to 63. I guess this brings me to the second principle of raises.

The Second Aim of a Raise: *The lower-paid faculty should have the impression they are catching up with the higher-paid faculty.*

Now for another raise strategy, again an extreme case.

(b) Across the board, equal dollar amounts.

It's hard to imagine circumstances in which this is appropriate. Though this is the dual to the previous strategy, it also violates both the First and Second Aim of a Raise.

(c) Devise a formula that incorporates a percentage raise that decreases with the size of your salary, a fixed dollar amount, and have the whole thing weighted by a merit index that is set by a small committee.

I've never been a fan of formulas outside of mathematics. I guess I have seen too many instances when a formula has been used as a veneer of objectivity to mask a purely subjective process. Actually, I lived for many years where raises were determined by a formula of this type. The formula changed from year to year in substantial ways. Besides the merit numbers there were other coefficients that came from the total amount of money in the raise pool. I really can't remember any of the formulas, except that every formula ended with "$+\epsilon$". I understood this; formulas are imperfect and the merit assessment process is imperfect. But what I didn't realize until many years later was that this took advantage of the mathematician's natural inclination to think that ϵ is positive and small; sometimes it was neither.

On more than one occasion during my life with a raise formula, when I made an effort to find out how the formula was constructed, I discovered that it was basically a curve-fitting process. The head took the merit numbers from the committee and came up with a formula that resulted in the raises that he believed were correct. Perhaps this is an argument that a formula in the hands of a mathematician can be a dangerous thing.

(d) Assign merit points to each faculty member, add the merit points for the entire faculty, divide the raise pool by this total number of merit points, and compute each faculty member's raise by multiplying his/her merit rating by this quotient.

This has a lot of virtues. It will satisfy both aims of a raise, unless there are lower-paid faculty who aren't accomplishing much. But for those people the two aims are in conflict, so don't worry about it. The merit points could be assigned by you or a committee, and this part of the work can be done even before you know the size of the raise pool.

It has an additional attribute. There are no penny ante differences in the raises. A source of constant criticism by faculty after a raise is the existence of $100 differences between two people. "How can you make a $100 distinction?" is a legitimate question. It's also one that seldom has a plausible answer. With this strategy raise differences are in multiples of a fixed, justifiable number.

There are several variations here. It is desirable that everyone get some kind of raise unless (s)he is a true hindrances to progress. You could give everyone a fixed number of points. Or you could subtract some amount from the raise pool and distribute this across the board as equal percentages or equal amounts.

Another variation is the dual of this strategy. First decide the total number of merit points. In effect this means you decide how much each merit point is going to be worth. This could be preceded, of course, by giving an across-the-board raise. Then you go about giving out all the merit points, either alone or with a committee. This tends to counter the basic flaw in this approach. Making distinctions between faculty is hard and has a certain surreal aspect to it. With time you may tend to start inflating the number of points awarded. By limiting the total number of points that can be given, you force yourself to make hard decisions.

(e) Gather information and opinions, see how this collates with your own opinions, and make a decision.

Gathering the information here takes some work. I have had a committee give each faculty member a number rating in each of the categories of research (R), teaching (T), and service (S). This usually works as follows. I give each member of the Advisory Committee a sheet with all the faculty listed in a column. On these sheets are three additional columns labeled R, T, and S. I tell them to give each of our colleagues (excluding themselves and me) a merit number between +3 and -3 in each of the three categories. The rule is that each column has to add up to 0, so no one is able to be overly severe or overly generous with the faculty as a whole.

When all the numbers are in, I massage them in various ways. For each of the three categories R, T, and S, I add all the scores given Professor X by the entire committee. This gives the committee's composite scores for Professor X. Then I add R + T + S for each

Professor X. I linearly order them, within ranks and across the faculty. I do this again with the numbers for one or more of the raters excluded, especially if I detect the possibility of unfairness. I want to emphasize that I do this in private and no one sees any of this massaging going on. The whole process takes me an evening (spreadsheets are marvelous). I print everything out and spend another evening looking at them.

Basically I look for consistency. Occasionally I see a member of the committee being out of synch with all the rest, and I try to figure out why. (Great fun.) This process manages to give me a picture of the committee consensus of who is and who isn't doing a good job. It has some drawbacks, which I'll discuss shortly.

I also pass out a copy of the composite numbers to the committee (with their own scores deleted), and we have further discussions. I am curious if anyone disagrees strongly with the committee's consensus.

I particularly remember one occasion when after giving the committee the composite figures, one member recoiled in horror and wanted to know if I was going to now translate these numbers into raises. I pointed out that this was like using a formula and I am opposed to that. "OK," he said, "but how are you going to use these numbers?" I tried to explain. I was sensitive to the fact that he and the committee had worked hard generating their numbers. I attach importance to them, but not in a deterministic way. They are a guide, not an itinerary. I worried that he might think I should give his/their opinion more weight. He responded, "A more appropriate approach is to throw the numbers in the trash and make up your own mind." I don't agree with that, but my opinion is closer to his than the use of a formula.

One difficulty with all these strategies is what I call "number abuse". The world is rife with it. Statistics and formulas are frequently used to lie and cheat while offering a sham of objectivity. As a department head you will be tempted to fall into this trap. People will ask you to justify your decisions. It is seldom that professional judgment suffices as an explanation, even though that is often why you are chosen to be head. Even with the educated, numbers have a more authoritative ring. I'll grant that prejudice and personal dislike often hide behind "professional judgment". And there have been many occasions when I used judgment and was accused of indulging my baser instincts.

As I said earlier, no raise strategy is going to be acceptable to all. No course of action is going to please everyone. So don't have this as an objective, whether you are deciding raises or whom to have lunch with. You have to decide on a policy that fits the situation and that you feel comfortable with and stick with it. Be fair. You'll do as well as you could hope.

(f) An across-the-board raise to all using a portion of the raise pool with some large quantum raises to a small fraction of the faculty.

This strategy has a special appeal when the raise pool is small. Suppose the raise is 2% (sadly, a too-frequent occurrence these days). You might take half of that and pass it around evenly and then award a fifth of your faculty with larger raises. Continuing with the 2% example (and a simplified model), this means four-fifths of the faculty get a 1% raise, and a fifth of the faculty get a 6% raise. For that fifth of the faculty, the raise has some impact. A 2% raise for all helps almost no one.

Of course those who do not belong to the blessed fifth will be put out and complain. You can explain your decisions, but in the final analysis you'll probably have to agree to disagree with the other four-fifths of the faculty. That's why they pay you the big bucks.

Before leaving this subject, let me say without equivocation that I am in favor of getting others involved in the rating process. You alone are incapable of going it alone, especially if you are at a research department. You only know your own research, so you can't expect to have an appreciation of everyone else's. Get others into the act. Even if yours is not a research department, are you really capable of correctly assessing the teaching of all your colleagues? Are you certain you are not biased in favor of a particular style of teaching? But the more who are involved, the less likely you are to make distinctions in quality. Democracy tends to level. So be careful not to turn this part of the process into a popularity contest.

There are places where soliciting of opinions about your colleagues breaks down, especially at a research university. The culture of mathematics tends to not value certain talents and contributions as they should be valued. In my own department, for example, I see many people getting a maximum research rating and hardly anyone getting the maximum in teaching or service. What about Professor Q, who has stopped doing research and is running the departmental computer network? How about Professor Z who is spending evenings devising a way to integrate the basic linear algebra and differential equations courses? Or Professor T, who had a personal fight with the preceding head, got a succession of low raises, but whose research and teaching is not so stellar as to get rave reviews from the committee? The head has to step in. Professors Q and Z are making contributions to the mission of the department, and you must recognize this no matter what the consensus is. Professor T deserves justice, and don't ever expect a committee to render justice; they may do this, but don't expect it.

§13. Retention, tenure, and promotion.

The three topics listed in the title of this section appear in order of importance. They are separate, and each has its distinctive aspects. Everyone knows what I refer to as tenure. Promotion here means promotion to full professor, as promotion to associate professor is usually synonymous with tenure. Retention means the retention, without granting tenure, of faculty who are on probation. I think I'll discuss these in the order in which someone encounters them in their career.

Before getting into the specific topics, a few words about this whole process. Personnel decisions are the core of the head's life and the basis for assessing his/her tenure in the job. Tenure, promotion, and retention decisions will reflect the head's judgment and sense of quality, both to the dean and to the department.

The quality of a tenure dossier will tell the dean a lot about your vision for the future of the department, irrespective of what you have written or said. Your ability to get the promotion through the channels will tell the department how effective you are and the extent to which they can rely on you. So be careful here. Having impossible standards will deflate departmental morale, and promoting with abandon will destroy your credibility. And once you have decided to back someone for tenure or promotion, go to it. In your report make him/her sound like the answer to a prayer.

But make no mistake about it. In tenure and promotion cases, it is not the candidate alone who is being judged. The head's judgment and effectiveness are being examined by the faculty and the dean, and the consequences of this are almost as important for you as the final verdict is for the candidate.

Each person's definition of quality will influence each decision. I would not start to try to set out criteria for excellence, especially since the definition of excellence in questions of personnel should be locally determined. In the final analysis, the department must answer the question: "Will this institution be better for having tenured or promoted this person?"

Retention.

The timing of a retention review seems to vary quite widely from department to department. Most universities require a yearly evaluation of probationary faculty. I believe that, to a large extent, this is legally motivated. If there were no review until tenure and tenure were denied, there would be a greater possibility of a lawsuit. If there are yearly reviews, the report of each review is positive, and then tenure is denied, the university is probably even more vulnerable to a court case.

Actually, I don't totally understand the basis for court cases here, save that employers simply cannot be capricious in their firing of people. I have been informed that the term "due process", as it appears in the United States Constitution, is a phrase that is often abused in public and academic discourse. It has nothing to do with the denial of tenure. Were you to fire someone who has tenure, due process enters, as the Constitution says no one can be denied life, liberty, or *property* without due process. A non-tenured job is not recognized as a property right, but tenure is. It used to be that capricious behavior by a university resulted, at worst, in censure by the AAUP. But the tendency is toward increased individual legal rights, so it is no wonder that the situation is as it is.

But forget about the legal question. If you wind up in court because you terminate someone, the university will furnish the lawyers. It will be a pain in the neck and consume a lot of time, but you'll have a whole new catalogue of cocktail party conversation topics.

In any case, a retention review is an important and useful procedure. On humanitarian and professional grounds, junior faculty should get a clear understanding of their status long before tenure is considered.

Assuming that a faculty member is hired with no credit toward tenure, (s)he will be considered for tenure at the beginning of their sixth year. In my department, we have yearly evaluations of probationary faculty done by the head, with a formal retention review in the fall of their third year. I take the yearly reviews seriously. I look at the publications and try to discern progress. I look at the teaching evaluations and the reports, if any, of the person's mentor. Recently my associate heads and I have begun visiting the classes of the assistant professors. Then I have a private meeting with each assistant professor and ask any questions I have about their performance. I also ask them to tell me how they feel they are progressing. I have not and probably never will terminate anyone after such a conference. I might conceivably order a formal review out of sequence if I detect a big problem.

The formal retention review in my department has a set structure defined in our bylaws. Letters are solicited and committees are formed to examine these letters and the candidate's research and to file a written report that is available to the tenured faculty. Similar committees are formed for teaching and service. Shortly before the faculty meet to discuss the case, a special committee, called the Recommending Committee, meets and votes on whether to recommend to the department the retention of the candidate. The decision of this committee is communicated to the junior colleague, who is invited to comment. Then the entire tenured faculty meet, discuss the merits of the case, and vote. It is my understanding that much of what I just described is fairly standard, except, perhaps, for the timing and the existence of the Recommending Committee.

In my experience, few faculty are ever terminated at a retention hearing. There is the rare case in which the untenured assistant professor has acted outrageously. Maybe (s)he has been involved in sexual harassment, missed classes, not had office hours, or has published nothing in the three years since (s)he was hired. But almost any hiring/interview process tends to make such cases rare. What happens more frequently, when the review is conscientiously performed, is that certain weaknesses are unearthed. Here is where the head must act like one.

It is the head's solemn duty to report to the candidate any bad news that comes out of the retention review. In a serious situation, the candidate should be asked to respond in writing. No one likes to communicate bad news. (Well, almost no one.) But it is absolutely essential that you do this, especially now. A head who puts on kid gloves at such a time is doing no one a favor. If the report is so bad that it seems irredeemable, terminate the candidate now before tenure is considered.

There is the legal question, but there is also your obligation as a human being and the unofficial mentor of this young colleague. Do you really want them to spend the next few years thinking there is nothing to correct? That what they have been doing is leading toward tenure? And meantime the faculty is anticipating change and will conclude, when it fails to appear, that this person did not heed a warning and, hence, is unworthy of tenure. I have known of cases where a department head did not pass on the faculty's concerns. When tenure was eventually denied, the candidate was shocked, the faculty discovered their warnings were not transmitted, and the head's prestige and reputation suffered.

What criteria should be applied to grant retention? Of course this depends on the mission of your department. But a good basic principle is that the young faculty member is meeting the expectations that you had when they were hired. Everyone must have a break-in period. Whether they are at a large research institution or a small liberal arts college, they will have a period of adjustment. In research they must make that transition from being under the tutelage of their major professor to independence. This may also be the first time they have had complete independence in their teaching. If they are from abroad, they will also have to adjust to the unique American university system. All this takes time and help.

There is the possibility that this review discovers a serious problem. When this has happened, I have informed the assistant professor that tenure was seen as problematic. There might be a chance for them to rectify the situation, but perhaps seeking another job would be the most prudent course.

Unless there has been a sharp, unexplained discontinuity in their performance, I think junior faculty should be retained until the tenure hearing. They should be alerted to various weaknesses, however. Do they give too many A's? Is their research production skimpy by local standards? Don't they have anything to say on committees? Why are the students complaining so much about their teaching?

Once the weaknesses are isolated, is there something the department can do to help them? If there is a weakness in the research, it is probably something they will have to work out on their own. Better be sure they have a healthy research program of their own before they are awarded tenure. But perhaps improved mentoring in their teaching duties will alleviate problems. You know, some very intelligent people can do weird things in the classroom and never be aware that what they are doing is weird and ineffective teaching.

Tenure.

Second to recruiting, tenure is the most important decision a department makes. Some may disagree with me and believe that tenure is more important than hiring, but I think all will agree that they are the two things that will have the most influence on a department's future. I give the nod to hiring in importance because once hired there is a tendency on the part of all involved to grant tenure. Denial of tenure causes cataclysmic upheavals in the department. Fissures appear that are not soon healed. When a junior faculty member is denied tenure, it means that failure has occurred for all involved: the head, the tenured faculty, as well as the unfortunate young man or woman.

The head and the faculty fail because they did not foresee that this person would not work out for the institution. Time, money, and effort have been invested and there is no pay off. It is of little wonder that everyone wants a tenure case to succeed. There may have been factors beyond the department's control, but this will not ease the sense of failure. If this happens frequently, the head has to stand back and assess his/her approach to recruiting. As I said in the section on retention, to the extent that the candidate was given no early indication of difficulties, the situation is exacerbated and the head is more culpable.

Different departments have different traditions and attitudes about the degree of involvement of the head in the tenure and promotion proceedings. In most universities and colleges the head makes a recommendation to the dean. There may be a faculty vote or a committee vote that is also sent to the dean, and perhaps the department is set up so that the head's recommendation is determined by this vote. There may be some small places, community colleges, for example, where the head is the only person who has input.

Now in cases such as mine where the head's opinion is paramount, there is a school of thought that the head should refrain from expressing opinions about the candidates until the faculty deliberations have concluded. The idea here is that the head should listen and not try to influence the outcome of the faculty vote. There is much to recommend this approach, and it seems rational and logical. I think it is dead wrong.

In my opinion the head should be completely involved at every step of the deliberations. To be sure, (s)he should listen and try to avoid reaching a premature conclusion (usually a hard task). But some of the possible consequences of silence are far worse than the ill feelings of some faculty who might believe you are throwing your weight around. Indeed, I think this is a case where the head must test his/her leadership.

If you are faced with a case in which you are in opposition to a majority of your faculty in a tenure case, there is a truly serious problem. Many departments require a two-thirds positive vote for tenure (a sane measure), and perhaps a candidate has a majority but not the required plurality. Nevertheless, you feel (s)he should be tenured. It would be far better in such cases if you had made your position completely clear and even politicked your colleagues to persuade them to vote the way you want. I have been there and it is hard; a time of maximum stress. I don't care what the situation is, this is hard sailing.

Usually such a situation will occur because a large fraction of the department disagrees with you on the quality of a candidate's research or teaching. Assessing research seems rather straightforward. You read letters of recommendation, look at the papers and where they are published, you get the opinion of the local experts. It could be that the local experts are being unfair or biased, but in this case you should be able to get the majority of the department to side with you on fairness. Perhaps there is a large group in the department that believes this person's research is an area that should not be represented. This is a far more serious issue to contend with. The research direction of the department should have been settled before the candidate was recruited. Of course the candidate could have changed the direction of his/her research since being hired; in this case I am not sure I would be willing to contradict my colleagues' judgment.

Assessing the quality of teaching is far more complex. (See "Improving teaching" in §6.) This is a much more likely point of disagreement. First, everyone regards himself/herself as capable of judging teaching, whereas in looking at research there is a built-in reluctance to judge outside of one's area of specialization. Second, the profession seems totally unprepared to judge itself on this issue. There are few good methods of gathering reliable objective evidence of good teaching other than student evaluations. I believe in the value of professional judgment. But of course there is a professional in every faculty member in the department. So this is a natural place for strong disagreement. Different people can look at the same evidence and come to a different conclusion. Once again, where human beings are concerned, solutions are seldom unique. Are the bad student evaluations a consequence of the candidate hating students or some correctable measure? Will the candidate improve? Are the candidate's other virtues compensatory for his/her lackluster performance in the classroom?

My advice, which I have begun to follow myself, is to become very active when tenure and promotion cases are being considered and, save in the absolutely clear cases, to interview your faculty about their opinions. Listen to them! Be prepared to change your mind if the arguments are sound. But if there are strong differences in the department and, after listening and judging the opinions of a good sample, your opinion focuses itself, begin to lobby your colleagues and persuade them to follow you.

It also seems to me that a reasonable criterion for tenure is a demonstration of excellence in at least one of the areas of research, teaching, and service. I would only support tenure based on excellence in service for someone who was specifically recruited for a service role — such as an outreach mathematician, for example. In the areas where excellence is not demonstrated, I require adequacy. (I used to use the word "competency", but this seems to have very negative overtones for too many people.) Of course this is all words unless you have good notions of what excellence means. Various university handbooks take a stab at making such things explicit, but finally it comes down to personal standards.

A word of caution here is advisable. With five or six years of contact, people can become very friendly. Sufficiently friendly that hard decisions are almost impossible. Remember you are running a department, not a club. Chumminess is not an area where excellence suffices for tenure. Nice young mathematicians do not invite harsh judgments, but your job, and that of your colleagues, is to promote the well being of the university. It is not to promote the sociability of the department.

One final question I ask myself when tenure is being considered is whether the department will be a better place with or without this person. During the 30 or so years that this person may remain on the active faculty, will they make a positive contribution to the improvement of the department's mission? This is really what giving tenure is all about. If there is nothing special about them, they are unlikely to ever justify this long range investment.

Promotion.

At many universities, promotion to full professor is an anachronistic enterprise. My attitude may be a result of being a mathematician; academics in other areas disagree with me to a greater degree than mathematicians do. In one especially important way, this promotion at my present institution has more significance than in my prior one: there is a very healthy raise attached to the event. At some universities there is no raise connected to this promotion, and I believe the only privilege that accrues to a full professor is the right to decide who else becomes a full professor.

Traditionally, I believe, promotion to the rank of full professor was an acknowledgment that someone had attained the stature of a mature and complete scholar. In science and mathematics, where some of the best work of a career is done near the beginning rather than at the end, this is a bit inaccurate. Maturity, yes; wisdom, yes; continuing research with the same fire, not necessarily.

At some universities the rank of full professor is considered the necessary status for direction of graduate students, though others can petition for the privilege. This is somewhat misguided by too strong an attachment to tradition. While I believe that it is in the interest of junior faculty not to get too involved in directing graduate student research, the years between the assistant and full ranks are fecund and rich with ideas, often beyond the capabilities of the faculty member to personally pursue. From that point of view it is a good time for doctoral students, but the time demands come at the worst period of the career.

A head ought to try to get all his colleagues to the full rank — eventually. But, frankly, this is not an issue for which I can conceive putting my job on the line. If something happens after tenure and productivity lapses, there may not be much you can do. In many departments there are faculty who have been associate professors for an extended period. Some of these are very active in the life of the department, others are not. The active ones contribute in a number of different ways that enhance the department's mission; they deserve more recognition than they get. A promotion would certainly reward them and let them know how much they are appreciated and how highly they are regarded. I even think the faculty would favor promotion for them. The difficulty is at the upper levels. Deans and promotion committees look at what is on paper; they tend to count things like papers and grants and speaking invitations.

All promotion and tenure committees are looking at people from all over the university or college. Usually they never see someone from their own area as they are recused from such considerations. Consequently they are led inexorably toward numbers and comparisons. Someone who has been in rank for an extended period comes to this group at a definite disadvantage, no matter how highly their departmental colleagues value them. Without the numbers, the committee has little more than your word to go on. In such a situation it is paramount for the head to make the case in no uncertain terms.

Also realize that faculty in the sciences tend to have far larger bibliographies than mathematicians. To the extent that mathematicians are regarded as scientists, this causes difficulties, especially for a marginal case. People in the physical and biological sciences cannot perform their research without grants, so they believe that no scientific research is worth anything unless it attracts external funding. The meaning of joint authorship in mathematics is probably unique in the academic world. All these factors call for attention by the head when making a case for promotion. When that case has a scholarly weakness, they make it a truly uphill battle.

§14. Recruiting. *

This is really where the head makes a mark. It is through recruiting that a department renews and improves itself. It is also through recruiting that the department experiences the most acrimonious internecine battles with the greatest rancor. A time when the head must be both adventurous and cautious. It is the best of times and the worst of times.

It is in the interest of each group in the department to advocate that each of its members who departs be replaced by someone in the same area. This is part of the human scene. When a vacancy occurs in the department, the head will undoubtedly take a similar position with the dean and argue that a mathematician must be replaced with a mathematician. But to follow this line is a plan for maintaining the status quo. If this had been followed by all departments, the

---

* This is a long section and probably too detailed for some tastes, especially those of veteran heads. It's important, however, and so I resisted the temptation to cut.

only room for mathematicians in new and developing areas would be from newly created positions. Vacancies as well as new positions must be examined in light of the department's needs and ambitions. Just because the department has a tradition of strength in barrelled locally convex spaces does not mean it must continue.

What about the national scene? Is there an area of mathematics in which your students receive inadequate preparation because you have no expertise on the faculty? Has an area developed that is producing some of the best PhDs? Maybe you should expand in that direction to take advantage of this.

There are several reasons why you might want to expand into a new area, not the least of which is to take advantage of some peculiar circumstance. Maybe a mathematician has a spouse with extreme allergies and you are located in an area with exceptionally low pollen counts. If hiring him/her would improve the quality of the faculty, it seems to me this is a good reason to form a new group. Almost all undergraduate courses can be taught by any mathematician. There are few reasons why teaching must dictate the area of a new hire. But be aware that expanding into a new area is politically sensitive and very expensive, since it implies that more than one position will be devoted to such an expansion. Marshal support for such a venture.

Whether it is a faculty meeting, an executive or advisory committee, or an informal canvassing by the head of the faculty, there should be a process to determine what area will be recruited. Whether the position is new or a replacement, whether the area is already represented or a new one, talk to your colleagues.

There are some schools that might claim they always simply advertise for a mathematician and never have debates about the area. If you examine the advertisements, many do not specify area. Some of these may be genuine, but I think most of these ads reflect the fact that the department has not had discussions about the area. Now it is impossible to truly compare two mathematicians that appear in a search when they have different research interests. So eventually there will be a debate over which area has the greater need, though it might be disguised as a debate about people.

When, as a young associate professor in the early 70's, I first became involved in a search, we advertised for an opening in mathematics, with no preference for area. We got about 300 applicants and were upset by this volume. More recently, in my first search as a head in 1990, we followed the same course. This time the number of applicants exceeded 800! Now there is no way any committee can process 800 applications. Probably 300 is an impossible number. Such a search, at some point, necessarily focuses on some limiting parameters. (In the meantime an enormous amount of secretarial, faculty, and candidate time has been wasted.) It may be that only people with postdoctoral experience are considered, but searches at this point often seem to limit themselves by focusing on areas. It really is much more efficient to limit a search at the beginning. So before you place the ad, discuss and decide what you want. Place the ad to properly reflect this. This saves a lot of mathematician time that can be better spent.

After my first search as head, we limited our searches by area. Most recently we have expressed in the ads a *preference* for people with postdoctoral experience. We still get applicants who are totally disjoint from what we are looking for. In such cases I immediately send them a letter telling them, in my most diplomatic style, that they do not fit the search. (I occasionally get replies from the rejected candidate castigating me for my bad judgment.) This process usually results in a candidate pool of between 100 and 150 applicants.

Another factor that influences a search is affirmative action (AA). There seems to be wide local variation in AA rules. I have heard so many comments about the difficulty of dealing with an AA office and meeting its requirements. It is a complaint that spans disciplines and universities. To be sure, when I became head, some represented the AA office to me as a logjam in the recruiting process. But these guidelines concern procedure and never dictate whom you should hire. In fact, this is a problem mathematicians are programmed to cope with. There are many algorithms that are more difficult to follow than AA procedures.

What causes difficulty for many is a desire to approach recruiting in a sincere but free way. "I am a person of good will without prejudice. Why do I have to jump through these hoops?" "How dare they tell me my business and imply that I would act dishonorably!" This simply adds to the stress of recruiting and accomplishes nothing except ill will. Realize that the AA office may be audited by the Department of Labor or some other legal authority. They must be ready to show they have followed the rules. The folks in the university AA office you will deal with are lambs compared with the government bureaucrat they might have to face. The rules they must comply with are at least as rigid as the rules that determine whether you have a correct proof.

You know there is also the possibility that some of your faculty may have social prejudices. I have never met an openly racist mathematician. I have met some who are misogynists who thought it cute to wear a pig pin bearing the letters "MCP*". I have had colleagues who referred to a female colleague they disagreed with as a "dingbat". It is more likely that this latter attitude of latent, recessive prejudice exists. Be prepared to confront this head-on.

I think it important to have diversity on the faculty, and AA guidelines are an ally in this. When we search, the guidelines tell us that when we encounter a female or minority applicant, we should give more leeway in the definition of what we are looking for. Suppose you advertise for someone in subnormal operators; a woman or African-American doing research in non-self adjoint operator algebras should be close enough to warrant serious consideration.

The search committee.

Most departments form a search committee to recruit. Since becoming head, I have appointed myself as the chair of the committee, regardless of the area being recruited. This was a departure from departmental tradition, and it is not standard at many universities. Why do I do it?

The question for me is, "Why isn't this universal practice?" As I have said before, recruiting is the number one activity for the head and the basis for determining his/her success. Most heads, including this one, are not familiar with either the area or the reputations of the experts in the area. So you really cannot read the papers or even fully comprehend the research statement of an applicant. Maybe this is the reason all heads are not the head of all search committees: a feeling of inadequacy.

But a lot of things happen in the search committee that determine the direction of the search or cause it to focus in a way that was never discussed before the search began. Unless you are present you will not be able to influence the final outcome. You will be a spectator like the rest of your colleagues. You are thus putting *your* reputation on the line and ceding control to others. For me this is inconceivable.

I also believe that, in general terms, the main duty of a head is quality control. How can I do this from the sidelines? Besides,

---

* Male Chauvinist Pig.

there are other things you should be looking for in addition to research accomplishments. Experts will look for expertise. By being an
active participant in the search committee, the head can also try to
exercise some influence in looking for the quality of the candidates'
teaching and their collegiality and whatever else is important for the
department.

I usually form a search committee consisting of two or three faculty besides me. Usually the members are experts, but I have on
occasion included someone whose research area is only tangentially
related to that of the search. This helps broaden the perspective of
the committee. In my searches we include a phrase like "Review of
applications will begin December 1 and will continue until the position is filled." This allows us legally to look at the applicants and
begin making decisions early.

Just before the Thanksgiving recess, the committee meets and
discusses generalities. How will we rate the files? (Score each, with a
highest of $1+$ = interview this person, to a lowest of 3 = an inappro-
priate applicant.) What is the timetable? (Let's try to have an offer
out by February 1.)

I urge my committee to begin reading the files on December 1
with the idea that just after the new year we will meet to start the final
deliberations. At this point I may not read the applications. If there
is only one search under way or if the search is in an area about which
I have opinions, I may read some. But often I let the committee do the
first screening. When all the committee members have read the files,
we meet and try to get a short list of about 20 applicants. Usually
I start by gathering the files of the applicants who have received a 1
from each reader. Then we look for those who have at least one 1.
We seldom have to go further to arrive at a respectable short list. We
also engage in some discussion about the short list, especially about
those who have gotten widely differing scores.

Don't be surprised if you encounter the Will Rogers syndrome
on the committee. Someone who never met a mathematician whose
research they didn't like. They are on every faculty. The guy who
rates 10 people with a $1+$; how can you interview 10 people? I told you
you would meet strange personality traits in this job. It's interesting
even if a bit silly.

At this stage, in just about every search we have had, there is
a committee member who wants to add someone whom they highly
regarded but felt constrained not to give a 1. There seem to be many

reasons for this. Maybe someone made it to the short list who they felt clearly inferior to this person. Maybe this is a student of a friend and it would be embarrassing to cut him/her from consideration at this point. Whatever the reason, we add them.

We contact everyone on the short list to inform them we have an interest in their application, to be sure they are still available, and, by implication, to invite them to add anything to their file. Shortly after this first winnowing, we inform the remainder of the pool that we will not be offering them a job. Usually this is done by postcard. This seems to irritate some applicants. As one of them wrote in reply, "I took all the time and effort to apply and all I get from you is a postcard." I sympathize with their tension, but a rejection by formal letter is probably equally disappointing. Recruiting is hard work and a time of stress for both the department and the candidates. As much as the department has at risk here, remember that the candidate has far more at stake. The press of departmental business forces a lot of economies and dictates that some niceties be shortened. It seems to me that a quick postcard is better than a delayed letter that would still be a form letter.

I have found it instructive to read the diary of Ed Aboufadel that appeared in *Focus*. In this Mathematical Association of America-sponsored series, starting in October 1992, Dr. Aboufadel describes his search for a position with his trials, disappointments, frustrations, and eventual success. It is important to understand the recruiting process from the viewpoint of the candidates. To this end you might also look at the Young Mathematicians Network (http://www.ms.uky.edu/~cyeomans).

I then read all the folders on this short list. I make notes and assign them grades. I also urge the committee to reread the files on the short list, especially any where the rest of the committee gave different marks than they did. After the few days needed for reading, we reconvene. Here we decide on an interview list and a backup list. Part of this format is dictated by AA rules. For a single position we will put between 3 and 5 people on the interview list. We put no one on this list that we would not be happy to have as a colleague, at least as far as we can judge from the file. Available funds act as a limiting factor here, though I have always been willing to come up with the money to interview as many as we want. But interviewing candidates is intensive work and places heavy demands on the committee members and their time. The more interviews we have, the longer it will be before we can make an offer. The secondary list consists of the next 5 or 6 candidates.

At this point we are required to file a Request to Interview form with the dean and the AA office. This can take a while, and we make an effort to stay on top of the administration to be sure this form does not languish on someone's desk. I believe that speed at this point is crucial. The stress has mounted with the candidates, and they may be contacted by other universities. So we make repeated phone calls to ascertain the status of this form. My secretary and my administrative assistant offer to transport the form from one office to another to avoid the delays of campus mail. You can be sure that none of these folks outside the department will share your sense of urgency.

In the meantime, we contact the people on our interview and backup lists and inform them of their status. We ask them not to accept an offer without first contacting us. We do not inform the other candidates on the short list. This is a point about which I might be rightly criticized. I worry about a disaster and not being able to get anyone from the first two lists. It has never happened, but it is possible.

The interview.

As soon as we determine whom we want to interview, and before we receive approval from the AA office to interview anyone, I send the prospective interviewees an email that goes something like this:

"Dear Professor Goesgift,

"I am pleased to tell you that the Differential Geometry search committee in the Mathematics Department has decided that you should be invited for an interview. Are you still available?

"I must make you aware of two facts, however. First, we are inviting several people for interviews, and there is only one position available. This is unfortunate, because we would be happy to have as colleagues all the people we will interview. Second, there is some paperwork that is required as part of the affirmative action procedures before we can formally invite you for the interview. I estimate this paperwork will take about a week.

"The offer we will eventually make will include the following ..."

I then go on to talk about the teaching load, start-up funds, research funds, and moving expenses. I also tell them a bit about the university and our computing facilities. When we get permission to invite people for an interview, I tell them to buy a plane ticket for a certain date. Sometimes this has to be adjusted because of conflicts. I try to get them to arrive on the afternoon of Day 0, interview on Day 1, and depart in the morning of Day 2.

Because of the bad experience of one of my own students, I never permit two candidates for the same job to meet each other here. I can't think of anything more gauche that could happen during a recruiting season. Candidates occasionally know each other and sometimes are even aware that each is being interviewed. That's unavoidable. But even so, I won't let them be on campus at the same time.

I also assign a host to the candidate, usually a member of the search committee. It is the host's duty to see that the candidate is met at the airport and delivered back there when they depart. They also organize a dinner and set up times when faculty can meet the candidate. Other parts of the interview, such as a meeting with the dean, are arranged by my secretary. The host shepherds the candidate during his/her stay or makes arrangements for a substitute if there is a conflict.

Another part of each interview is a session with my administrative assistant. She goes over the fringe benefits, gives them information on housing, and, for the foreigners, ascertains their visa status and any possible difficulties that may arise should they be offered the position.

In my initial letter to the interviewee I also try to impart some of my personal approach to recruiting and a bit of a plea.

"It is my style to be completely honest with people (a policy that sometimes causes me difficulties). The academic world has its share of dishonesty and secrecy, and ultimately this behavior results in more difficulties than it avoids. I would ask that you be open and aboveboard with me. My experience is that in such stressful business as you and I are about to embark on, everyone will be better off if we can communicate in an atmosphere of openness and frankness."

I mean this. Over the years different candidates have manifested varying degrees of stress, but all have had some. I am enough of a realist to know that this request for openness won't always work. Candidates have an enormous amount at stake. This involves the rest of their lives. The department gets another chance to re-evaluate its decision at tenure time. True, candidates could look for other jobs later. But the realities of the present job market make this almost impossible; at the least it is not something anyone wants to do. So they are certain to act in their self-interest. It is very likely they will withhold something from their discussion with me. I want to set a tone, nevertheless. I want them to realize that I mean everything I say. Of course, having made such a statement, I had better live up to it. Few are so cynical as to ignore hypocrisy when discussing their employment.

A private conversation between me and the candidate lasts about a half hour, sometimes longer. Mostly I try to sell the department as a place to work. I do try to delve into the candidate's personality. Shy? Confident? Ambitious? There isn't anything particular I am looking for. Departments are so diverse, especially the big ones like those I have been associated with. There is room for a wide variety of personalities. I have a great curiosity about people, and I'd like to know something about someone we interview besides the papers and teaching experience.

I also discuss salary and other interviews they may have had or are about to have. In fact these are just about the first things we discuss. I do it in a straightforward manner, just as I promised in my letter. I ask them if they have other offers or interviews. I ask them if they have an idea about what salary they want. (Most do not, unless I mention a figure that is too low.) I also tell them that if we offer them the job, I will not lose them because of salary. I have been fortunate in having a dean who professes this; I take him at his word and have not been disappointed.

Part of my pitch to candidates is that I work to help all my junior colleagues become the best mathematicians they can be, both in research and teaching. Maybe this sounds corny. But I have seen too many places where junior faculty are abused. I have had colleagues who essentially abuse new faculty. There are senior faculty who believe the proper role of an assistant professor is to do their dirty work. My early career prospered from the help of several colleagues. It was an important part of my development.

I back my position up with an offer of lighter teaching loads for the first two years (one course a semester the first year, two courses one semester and one course the other during the second year, the standard two courses each semester after that). I also set aside a small stipend for research support during their first two years (travel and/or inviting seminar speakers and collaborators). This is in addition to start-up funds to buy a computer and peripherals. We don't carry a lot of prestige, but we can offer folks a rewarding and satisfying professional life (all in the shadow of Smoky Mountain National Park).

Before they leave I make sure they understand that we are interviewing others, when the interviews will end, and when they can expect to hear from me. I let them know that they will hear from me even if what I have to say is bad news.

One of the central parts of the interview is the colloquium talk given by the candidate. As a device for learning something about the candidate's teaching ability, it is limited. Someone who gives a really good talk helps his/her case, no doubt. You can get some idea how (s)he lectures. But lecturing in a class that meets three times a week is a far cry from giving a single talk on the mathematics you have created and lived with for the last couple of years. In my letter describing the interview, I discuss the talk as follows.

"As part of the interview process you will be required to give a 50-minute lecture to the faculty. It would be good if you could spend the first 20 minutes or so giving some background and setting your work in some historical perspective. In other words, show that your problem is related to the work of others. Remember that the audience will have varied backgrounds and, with a few exceptions, will lack expertise. It is of course important that you state and explain your own work. But also you should avoid becoming too technical. A lecture consisting of about 20 minutes of background together with some well-chosen examples, 20 minutes devoted to a statement of your results and an explanation of what it means and why it is important (which can often be demonstrated by stating some corollaries or a pertinent example), and then 10 minutes for an indication of the proof directed to the more expert members of the audience is usually the foundation of a successful colloquium. If you have to choose whether to give an example or some details of the proof, give the example. These are very broad guidelines and clearly some material calls for their violation. Discuss your colloquium talk with your advisor or a friend."

First, you would be amazed how many candidates do not discuss the interview colloquium with their advisor. Second, I think what I said is good advice for any colloquium speaker, not just one who is interviewing. Third, I have been criticized for hampering speakers from getting more deeply into their results — criticism I flatly and totally reject. Anyone can stand at the head of a room for 50 minutes and delve into technical details of their latest result. If, on the other hand, I hear a talk that follows the suggestions I made above and hear it done well, I have the idea that this is someone who not only has mastered the technicalities of his/her subject but really knows what it is about. This is someone with perspective, judgment, and taste. This is someone who is less likely to burn out before their career is 10 years old and who is more likely to be successful in the classroom.

If you think that letting them talk with no instructions would constitute a test, you might consider what it is that this would test. A less-involved thesis advisor? Naiveté? Inexperience? You surely are not testing teaching or research.

The dynamics of the interview is interesting to observe. There are people who help themselves with the interview, some hurt themselves, and some remain an enigma. I personally feel better hiring someone who has had a good interview. Candidates who have improved the way they are considered because of the interview have done so because they have interacted with the faculty, given a good talk, and been pleasant human beings. All of these are desirable traits in a future colleague. Presumably their research was highly regarded before they were invited, so we are not talking about diminished expectations there.

Making the offer.

After the interviews are concluded, the search committee meets to decide who should be offered the position. In some departments, like my former institution, it may be the entire faculty. If it's the entire faculty, my sympathy. My experience is that such decisions are best made by a small group. If the faculty is small, fine. But with 30 or more members, this can easily degenerate into a free-for-all. Even in a small committee the discussion can become quite lively. In a recent search a committee of four, including me, debated seven hours with an overnight break before coming to a decision.

The policy and tradition in my department say that I have the right to stop debate and make a decision. Actually, this would probably be easier in a discussion by the entire faculty rather than in a small group of three of my colleagues. In any case, it is a right I have so far avoided exercising. The committee has worked hard and conscientiously. To stop debate prematurely would be a betrayal. Since I am not usually an expert, I am reluctant to impose a solution to this problem.

In the particular case I mentioned above, involving a seven-hour debate, where all the candidates had made a good impression, I felt I was learning something from all that discussion. In fact the crucial event in the deliberations of that search committee came during the overnight break when members made phone calls to fellow experts and a member read through a couple of papers by a candidate. Everyone was acting in good faith, it was a good committee, and no one was being obstreperous.

So finally a decision is reached, hopefully within a couple of days of the last interview. At my university we need to file a Request to Make an Offer form. This is rather routine with a turnaround of about 36 hours. In the meantime I am on the email and/or phone making an offer "subject to final approval by the dean." I state the salary, teaching load, etc. And there is also the cruncher.

I impose a very quick deadline for a response. This is not a surprise for the candidate as we have discussed this during the interview. My position is that if (s)he has committed to an interview before I make an offer, I am bound to respect this and not place him/her in an awkward position by requiring a response to my offer before the other interview is completed. But I require a response within 72 hours of my making the offer or the completion of the other interview.

This is shocking to some, and I concede that it verges on "playing hardball". If I were the head of one of the top dozen and a half mathematics departments in the country, I might be more liberal (96 hours?). But I am not. We have a lot of assets here, and I think we have much to offer young mathematicians. We are also efficient. We do not keep the candidates dangling on a string while we leisurely make up our mind who we want to hire. We act quickly and decisively. (During the interview I underline this aspect of my headship as a benefit of being in this department. But, alas, they are too young to realize how important this is for their future.) The 72 hours together with whatever time has elapsed between their interview and our making the offer is sufficient to decide if they want to join us. Further delays only go toward letting other departments get their act together and make a counteroffer. I do not want to suffer because someone else is less efficient than we are.

I have occasionally extended the deadline, usually for a day or so if there are strange circumstances. I have yet to be successful in these circumstances. I don't really regret these extensions, because I don't want someone here who doesn't want to be here. There have been a couple of times I significantly extended the deadline. In one case, early in my career, I was just too soft. The candidate had a spouse who had a PhD (not in mathematics). He said she needed time to look into career possibilities in Knoxville, and I listened to this as a reason for the extension. Of course this was not mentioned until after the offer was made. (By the way, this was his right, and you have no right to ask a candidate if his/her spouse is also looking for employment. The official word here is that if employers know this is a consideration, they might not be as favorable to the candidate, as this might represent more trouble. It is more trouble, but something I am willing to do if I want this person for my faculty.) It didn't take long for me to regret giving this extension.

In the other case where I did not stick to a tight deadline, I felt totally comfortable doing so. We had the search, and one candidate emerged as extremely desirable to a large portion of the faculty, but somewhat less so to the true experts. This desirable candidate was coming off a successful two-year postdoc and had several interviews lined up after ours; he would not be able to give us an answer soon. We knew the competition was stiff. What to do?

I am ambitious. I want to significantly improve the quality of my faculty. During my first search at Tennessee, we had many good candidates in for interviews. People complimented me on the quality of the pool. I was also told by a couple of colleagues that I might be shooting too high and running the risk of getting no one. A more "realistic" approach was advised. Well the various reasons that made me become a head made this "realistic" approach totally unrealistic. It also made trying for the extra-good candidate an attractive option for me. (In that first search, by the way, I recruited our first choice.)

Again, what to do in that other search. The candidate who was next on our list, and first on the list of the experts, was a brand new PhD with a lot of promise as well as many other virtues. We were confident he would develop into a very attractive colleague. Whereas the veteran had several interviews yet to come, the fledgling had none. Aha! you say. Make the offer to the veteran; it is likely that the neophyte will still be available when the former postdoc has to decide. This certainly crossed my mind. But it is a bit too manipulative for my taste.

So we made the offer to the new PhD, and I marched up to the dean's office with the postdoc's file and asked for a second position with the proviso that if this candidate said no, the position would revert to the college. He agreed. I made the offer and was most generous about the deadline. (I had nothing to lose.) I even extended it once, though at that point I strongly suspected we would not be successful. We weren't.

One point about the preceding story that deserves emphasizing is that you will never get anything unless you ask. There have been several times that colleagues have told me I was wasting my time asking for certain items. In some of these cases I was unsuccessful, but in others I got what I asked for.

When I make the offer, I also contact the other people interviewed, as I said I would, and tell them the news. Another reason for a quick deadline is that I do not want to lose other candidates on our list. With each delay it is more likely that the second choice will go elsewhere.

There are interviews where five minutes after the conversation begins, I realized we will never hire this person. The candidate just sits there, asking no questions and seeming bored and disinterested. Sometimes they destroy themselves during their talk. In one case we discovered that the letter writers had vastly overstated the importance of the candidate's research. (Shame on us for not realizing this before the interview.) But almost always, everyone we interview is desirable. So there really is too much at risk to dawdle while a cautious candidate tries to reach a decision.

Postmortem.

After the offer is accepted, I try to have a postmortem. Usually I invite the search committee over to my house on a beautiful Knoxville day, I open a bottle of champagne, and we sit out on the patio basking in the sunshine and our glory. It's a good occasion. We also talk about the search, what we did right (lots to talk about there), and what we did wrong (not too much — after all, look how successful we were). This is helpful to me for the next search. I am a firm believer in self-analysis, and this is a group therapy session.

Possible problems.

The recruiting season can present several difficulties. I have been spared the monumental difficulty where the search is terminated by the administration after it has begun. This has always struck me as a sign of incompetence. Deans and chancellors are supposed to be able to read the messages that come from the fund sources and plan accordingly. Telling a department that a search cannot get started is unfortunate, but it indicates that they are doing their job. If the approach is conservative, you are still better off in the long run. If a search is cancelled after the process has begun, the department suffers great humiliation. Maybe this would still be a time to open the champagne, or something stronger, and pray for deliverance.

If you are recruiting good, new PhDs, it is quite likely that someone you offer the job to will also receive some type of postdoctoral temporary appointment. If you can, let them take it. I have a standing offer to anyone we hire that if such an offer arises, they can accept for one year. This has happened, and in such cases the first year of their appointment is a leave without pay. There is the possibility that they will not show up, but I don't think it likely.

This happened to me once. I gave the man we hired a leave of absence in his first year, and he didn't show up the next year-almost literally. He was from abroad, spending the year in the US. He told me he felt an obligation to return to his home institution. He felt no such obligation towards us. Less than four weeks before the semester began, he sent me an email message that he had been offered a promotion and was going to stay.

The other times it has worked out. A postdoctoral position has benefits for a career far beyond the year or so they last. The intense research activity after the thesis is synergistic. After that year you get a better faculty member who salutes your generosity and wisdom.

A problem that can arise during the search that is more serious is faculty speaking out of turn. Every department has members who are disgruntled. Don't be too surprised if one of these begins talking to the candidate, and they parade out their unhappiness and complaints. Try to avoid this, if possible; don't invite such faculty to meet the candidate. If the candidate talks to such faculty, confront this head on. Don't wait for the applicant to mention what (s)he heard. They may never talk about it and go away with a false impression.

§15. Perquisites and travel.

One person's perquisite is another's due. Professional personalities are as varied as students. Some of your colleagues will almost never ask for anything; others will seem to have set up camp outside your door. It's just something you have to deal with and dealing with it well is important.

You do realize you have perks to give out, don't you? Offices, for example. Everyone needs one, of course. But how big? How about the location? Then there are computers. Some faculty use computers in their research; I'm not talking about them. For mathematicians who use a computer to do research, this is not a perk. Of course colleagues who don't use a computer for research but do all their own word processing relieve the workload on the staff and increase efficiency — probably a good investment.

I'm someone who believes that people should have more computer power than they need. In general people's computer usage tends to expand to fill their computer's capabilities. That's good. But there are many decisions involved with approving the purchase of computers for faculty that are more a question of convenience and timeliness than necessity or efficiency. This puts these decisions in the realm of awarding perquisites rather than supporting research and scholarship.

I am going to discuss travel here even though it really is not a perk. In the business community travel often is a perk. People go to conferences where there are sessions in the morning, which may or may not be attended, and then the afternoon is free for golf or sightseeing. Often travel to such "conferences" is a perk that corporations give out to loyal and productive employees. Doctors have discovered such travel as a tax-deductible method of having a vacation. It is no wonder that many in the public tend to regard travel by university personnel as a perk. If the university is tax supported, overseas travel can cause incredible outrage on the part of the taxpayers. In fact, the travel I have done for academic purposes has been hard work.

I am discussing travel here because it is something the head can use to promote certain activity and to encourage some faculty to pursue activities (s)he sees as worthy. Even though it is not a perk, it does have many of the aspects of a perk in that faculty regard travel support as a reward, even when they feel it is a necessary part of their profession.

For many department heads this is not a controllable item. In some universities travel grants are dispensed by the dean; in some universities there is no travel sponsored by the institution (except the travel of the dean). In mathematics and most academic departments travel is an important ingredient in making a successful program. There is research travel; it's important for your faculty to find out what is going on in their discipline. On the other hand it seems to me that in recent years we have seen an explosion of conference activity, often with partial support for participants. And of course the best researchers often have research grants that support travel.

There is also travel that will enhance the teaching in the department. What is the latest development in teaching reform? What

experiences have others had with combined differential equations and
linear algebra courses? How useful is Maple for precalculus? For this
type of travel there is very little external support and conferences are
rare.

There is also some travel the head should do as a head, beyond
what (s)he does as a researcher or teacher. Some heads travel to
AMS/MAA meetings for recruiting. This is the public's main notion
of travel by the head. Even though the head can give an initial screening of candidates, I've never been a big advocate of this. I usually
have enough to do at these meetings without tying up a large block
of time meeting a collection of candidates. But if your department
has only a small budget for campus interviews, this may be a very
efficient process and worth sacrificing some time you might spend at
research or teaching sessions.

Then there is the National Chairs Colloquium in October in
Washington, DC. The first of these that I attended was in my first
year as head; it was most useful. The second one I attended, in my
fourth year, was less so. These colloquia are organized around a central topic; some topics will clearly have more appeal than others. Like
similar smaller or regional meetings of heads, the National Chairs Colloquium gives you an opportunity to see what others are doing on the
job, and you may learn something to carry home. The quality and
value of these varies greatly, just like research conferences.

In Tennessee we have an annual meeting of mathematics department heads from the state-supported colleges and universities — from
the University of Tennessee to the community colleges. We meet from
Friday noon to Saturday noon at a geographically varying site. We
just sit around a table and discuss our difficulties and accomplishments. We talk about being more involved in trying to influence
statewide policy, but so far it's just talk. I find it interesting and
useful (more than I initially anticipated). A lot of what happens is
similar to the functioning of a psychological support group. I advocate
creating such a group if one doesn't already exist in your area.

How do you decide who gets the special perks? I'm not sure I
have a set answer, but I am inclined to say it should be similar to the
process of deciding who gets what size raise. Hard workers should get
your support and the sloths and moribund should not. Reward the
virtuous and punish the wicked.

I do know what to avoid. Don't just give out the perks to your
friends. It is difficult, but you have to put the good of the department

and the profession ahead of your personal likes and dislikes. A hard working s.o.b. should be taken care of before a lovable, good-natured pal whose main contribution is his/her ability to give sparkle to conversations about compost piles. If you start making such decisions on a personal basis, you are probably setting the stage for your departure from office in disgrace, and you will deserve all the ill will you receive.

§16. Staff.

Good staff is one of your most valuable assets. Treasure and nurture them. If they are happy and efficient, you will be happy and efficient. Your faculty will bless you if the secretaries are professional and willing to help them with their work; otherwise they will curse you or, worse, tsk-tsk you as a bumbler. So getting, training, and keeping good staff is a very important part of what you will do for the department. It is also an aspect of the job that is most unfamiliar to academicians, one for which we are not prepared.

In most large departments there is usually someone designated as administrative assistant or business manager or office manager. Smaller departments often have a secretary who fills a similar function. If you don't have such a person, try to get one. Make it a condition of employment if you can. Either create a new position or upgrade someone on the staff who will accept these responsibilities. A good administrative assistant will mean the difference between your having an enjoyable and successful term as head and having a term filled with frustration and failure.

I say this with the full realization that in very small departments having an administrative assistant is not possible and secretarial support may be so meager as to preclude having someone function in this way. Of course, in a smaller department there may not be as much to contend with in the daily routine of managing the office. But the head needs to concentrate on mathematical issues. So if it is possible, leave the office and staff problems to someone else to concentrate on. Besides, you probably don't know how to handle staff. Few of us have had any experience here.

If you already have an administrative assistant and (s)he is deficient, go for a replacement. Ask the dean for help; (s)he has probably been in administration for awhile and knows the ropes. If you have to get ruthless, do so. Most universities have definite, inflexible rules about firing people (a good thing most of the time). But start the process. Write letters of reprimand. File bad performance reports. Openly tell the administrative assistant of your intentions to get rid of him/her; they may get the message and quit. It will be better to go through pain and agony for a year or so than put up with the administrative assistant from hell throughout your term of office. It is not inconceivable that replacing a bad administrative assistant will be regarded by your colleagues as one of the accomplishments of your term.

An efficient, well-run office will result in a better department. Papers and letters need to be typed, grants need to be budgeted and administered, faculty projects need to be expedited. Organizing a conference requires a lot of secretarial assistance. If you want these things done and do not want to be personally involved (you shouldn't), then be sure there is staff that is capable and efficient. The best way to guarantee this is not to do it yourself. The best way is to have someone who has the direct responsibility for seeing that it comes to be. This is what I call an administrative assistant. You will have faculty to deal with, curriculum to oversee, deans to negotiate with, and scholarship to pursue. Get an administrative assistant. (Have I made myself clear on this point?)

A good personal secretary is also essential. Early in my career as department head, a budget cut dictated that we had to lose a secretary. My own secretary had a line on another job she considered a step up and she got it. I decided to just share a secretary with my associate heads. It was a mistake.

A year later my administrative assistant came to me and said, "You MUST have a secretary." Her knowledge of office dynamics and the clear recognition that my lack of a personal secretary was impeding my work, as well as her own, convinced her there was no other way. (Another benefit of a good administrative assistant.)

The administrative assistant reorganized the staff (that secretarial position that disappeared in the budget cut never reappeared) and promoted one of the secretaries in the office. I got a true gem of a secretary, and my performance as head improved; the whole department is better off. This also resulted in my having more time to devote to scholarship and the needed planning for the department.

Make an effort to help the staff to develop and prosper. This entails encouraging them to take classes if they choose and to acquire new skills. It also means fostering an atmosphere of mutual respect between the faculty and staff.

The secretaries have to know what their jobs are. They have to know that faculty will need assistance in a variety of tasks. Students need to be addressed and helped courteously and promptly. The faculty has to understand that even though they may put in 10-hour days and not leave the building until 6:30 pm, secretaries have set hours. (So don't allow faculty to show up with a rush typing job at 4:45.) If any colleague screams or is similarly disrespectful of the staff, you or your administrative assistant must let him/her know that such behavior is reprehensible and cannot continue.

Another type of staff that is becoming part of the scene is computer support personnel. This is another problem I had to confront early in my term. The first day I arrived on campus, a very costly contract, roughly $26,000 in 1990, with the UTCC (University of Tennessee Computing Center) for technical support of the Sun network was on my desk waiting for approval. I was aghast. The Sun network had fewer than 25 machines then, and this contract covered backups, installation, advice, etc. There was a separate contract for maintenance.

Closer investigation revealed that everyone on the Sun network was dissatisfied. Some faculty were no longer using their Suns because the network was too slow and crashed too often. I talked with UTCC, eliminated some services, and they reduced the bill. I also set about finding a better solution. For the amount of money the contract costs, I reasoned, we can hire our own person.

I was right and I was wrong. A year later, at the conclusion of the contract, we hired a student who had experience as a UNIX system administrator (USA); the student worked part time. Things improved. The student graduated. I hired a full-time USA. This was a person who talked so much, I began to suspect all that talk was a smoke screen to mask something. I was right. Things deteriorated. I got another administrator. Things improved. I got the university to upgrade the position. The system has stabilized, but the USA position has not.

People to administer computer networks are in high demand. Many of these who purport to know UNIX do not. Our Computer Science Department has a USA who handles a much larger network than ours, and they pay considerably more. We seem to be in a pattern of getting very good people, but we cannot keep them. We are paying something more than the original UTCC bill, and the system has grown to over 35 machines. My impression is that to get stability you need to pay about one-and-a-half times what we pay. (I am not certain of this.) Since that is comparable to a faculty salary and since I don't have that kind of money in my budget, I have to live with the instability.

We are getting to a situation where we can get very good people for computer support paying lower than market wages because we are a university. We do have better fringe benefits (the health care is the important item here), and there are very talented people who want to work for us. Perhaps they want to complete a degree or their spouse does. Maybe they just like the university atmosphere. Eventually they are going to move on. If we can go two years between USAs, I figure we won't suffer too much. Well, I can't control the pain and suffering, so I'll just say that we won't suffer too much.

In addition to the Sun network, we have a Novell network that links our Macintoshes and PCs. The manager of that network is a faculty member. This faculty member is no longer interested in doing research but had become very interested in computers. Early in my career as head he approached me and asked to take a bigger role in departmental computing. (See §7.) He does an excellent job and makes a significant contribution to the department.

This faculty member had no training or experience in network managing when he began, but he is a smart guy. (He has a PhD in mathematics, after all.) He has taught himself a lot, and I have sent him to some workshops and meetings where he has learned more. It has been a good investment. He manages this network and runs our computer lab, which includes supervising our lab assistants. He has also become very useful at implementing meaningful computer work in the classroom.

If you have a faculty member who is interested in working with computers, this seems like an optimal solution of a hard problem.

We also have a cadre of students who work in our lab and assist the network manager. They are smart, energetic, and excited about their work. We try to keep them employed during the summer, where they run the lab and help out the manager. We pay something close to minimum wage, but this is better for them than flipping burgers.

§17. People vs Institutions.

I have said several times already that the head's job is to improve the department and thereby the university. So what I am about to say is somewhat contradictory.

It is more important to have loyalty to people than to institutions. Like all one-liners, this needs some explanation to be fully understood. I certainly don't advocate blind loyalty to anyone or anything. Some people and some institutions don't deserve anyone's loyalty.

The reconciliation of the two seemingly contradictory statements lies in the premise that you advance the department by contributing to the advancement of the people in the department. Another one-liner that somewhat captures the spirit: the head should represent the department to the dean and not represent the dean to the department. Help the faculty and the department will improve.

Remember that institutions have short memories and seldom show any loyalty to people. It is also true that universities seldom do much to encourage loyalty. Let's face it. Most universities are too big to foster any sense of community. Departments are another matter. They are smaller, and there is often a sense of identification by faculty and staff with the department. This is especially true if the head treats the people well.

What are some specifics? A colleague comes to see you in late April and says (s)he has an offer of a visiting appointment at MRIA (Mathematical Research Institute of Appalachia) for the coming year. Granting a leave this late means it is unlikely you will be able to find a temporary replacement. I think you should do your utmost to grant the leave. This leave will be more important for the colleague than any temporary inconvenience for the university. If the department is small and this faculty member's absence would result in cancelling a course vital for the coming graduating class, then this is a different situation. But I would move heaven, earth, and the rest of the faculty's schedule to try to enable the leave. Some of the other faculty might resent this. But they should realize that you would do the same for them and in the long run they will appreciate your sticking up for their colleague.

One of your most important faculty asks you to write a letter of recommendation in support of his/her application for another job. Write the best letter you can. (I think few would disagree with me on this point.) If (s)he is offered the job, do your best to persuade the university to make a counter offer that cannot be refused. Even if you fail, the rest of the faculty get a clear message of where your loyalties lie.

A secretary comes to you and requests permission for several days off to attend a workshop to learn the use of a computer spreadsheet and some other software packages. Offer to pay the registration fee. This is a non-traditional use of department funds (unfortunately) and some faculty may complain, but you'll gain a secretary with increased loyalty and additional skills. The department will suffer a few days of diminished help; you'll have to dig out the money from some nook or cranny. But this will be a globally beneficial act. Also the staff will get a strong message of your concern for them.

So the guiding principle here is to do what you can to promote the careers and professional development of your faculty and staff, even if it means an inconvenience for the university. If they prosper, so will the department, so will the university.

§18. Nominating colleagues for honors.

I know of mathematics departments where no one has ever been nominated for a teaching award. This contributes to the department's having a reputation on the campus for bad teaching. Of course many mathematics departments have this reputation, and it is usually undeserved. (I have discussed some of the reasons for this already in §6.)

You should take the plunge. Go ahead and nominate your colleagues for teaching and research awards. OK, both Professors Alpha and Omega as well as half a dozen others deserve the award, and you can (should) only nominate one. Make a decision! Nominate Professor Alpha this year. Professor Omega will have to wait until next year. If this upsets Professor Omega, talk to him/her. Explain that you had to choose, it was close, and whether A does or does not get the award this year, you will nominate Omega next year. If Omega is still upset, keep working on him/her. Hopefully Omega will come around, but if not, this is not the kind of thing that will cause a disaster in the department. In fact, if Omega is just totally bananas about being asked to wait a year, maybe (s)he is not as worthy as you originally thought. (This presumes you didn't handle the explanation in Neanderthal fashion.)

Taking positive steps toward recognizing your colleagues' accomplishments will have a far larger effect than you might imagine.

§19. Meeting outside offers.

Professor Grantsglut informs you that (s)he has an offer from another university. What should you do? Of course many factors will influence the answer. How good is Professor Grantsglut? How good is the other university? Is the offer for a professorship, or is it for a headship and thus a career change? Is the offer in writing? Why not?

When someone comes to you with an outside offer, your leadership and judgment are on display. It's a crucial time. The dean and the entire faculty are looking and will judge your actions. Be wise.

As head I have had only one colleague come to me with an outside offer. I wanted very much to retain him, but I knew from the start that I would probably fail. He told me so. But I fought, nevertheless. If nothing else, by trying to keep him I sent a message about my priorities to my colleagues.

While a faculty member I knew several mathematicians who got outside offers, and I myself had a few. Many colleagues regard such an offer as a ploy to get an increase in salary. Though external offers are sometimes a maneuver undertaken to improve salary and other benefits, it is a mistake to regard them as such. Part of the reason an external offer is so regarded is jealousy. When Professor Grantsglut informs you of his/her offer, you may even experience some jealousy yourself. Try not to let it cloud your judgment. (How easy to say, how hard to observe.)

Universities have poor mechanisms for rewarding the productive, especially when democracy is a strong component of its governance. As I mentioned in §11, democracy tends to level all, especially where salaries are concerned. This leads some to frustration and a sense that they are not appreciated. When faculty feel unappreciated and seek or entertain an outside offer, they may do so because they want to change universities or to leverage their current department into recognizing their worth. There are some indicators that might point to this latter scenario. The other university might be decidedly inferior to your own; this particular faculty member may have a history of frequently gathering external offers. (Frequent offers do not just happen; they are solicited.) But even in such a situation, dismissing this offer is done only at the risk of losing the colleague. It might even be that your colleague enters your office hoping for a raise and not wanting to leave. But if your reaction is tantamount to an insult, if you fail to take this seriously, you may be telling him/her good-bye.

Exactly how to react to an outside offer depends so much on the particular circumstances. Initially I would congratulate my colleague on the external recognition and tell him/her I want to consult with other faculty about an official response. This is a good course of action. Even if, deep down, you want to be rid of this pain in the neck, take this tactful position. You could caution that a counteroffer might be a problem. In no case, however, should you display optimism. Remember that this colleague is in a very emotional state with a psyche that is in high gear. It is quite likely that anything but the most straightforward statement will be misinterpreted.

But let's assume that Grantsglut is a good researcher, a good teacher, and a desirable colleague — someone you definitely want to keep. The offered salary is a 20% raise, further evidence (s)he is a desirable commodity. Do you match the salary? Maybe you can succeed by countering with only a 15% raise. Again there are no hard rules. Is Grantsglut particularly sensitive? Will (s)he be upset with the gamesmanship implied by a smaller counteroffer? Is the risk of offering less worth it? The head has to be cautious and wise. Matching the salary is likely to raise the hackles of the rest of the faculty. If this is a big concern, you could give a smaller salary and throw in an extra stipend for each of the next three years to facilitate Grantsglut's research. To the extent that salary is a form of recognition, an unusual thing like research funds might imply greater recognition than extra salary. Talk to the rest of the faculty as well as the dean and Professor Grantsglut. But never lose sight of your final objective: you want Grantsglut to stay.

As I said, giving Grantsglut a raise will upset some on the faculty. I don't care how good you think (s)he is, others will disagree. This is a reaction that freely mixes professionalism and jealousy: your colleagues may not see their jealousy, and you may not see their professionalism (either of which may not be there). But given the fact that you want to keep him/her in your university, you must do what you have to do. You may be criticized, but you are following your vision of what is best for the department. That's your job.

Another emolument that is frequently used is the reduced teaching load. I am opposed to offering anyone a lifetime teaching reduction. We have tenure, and one lifetime contract is enough for anyone. A commitment of a reduced teaching load for five years with review and possible renewal seems a better course to me. Too much changes over time. There is nothing like an older, no-longer-productive colleague with a special privilege to congeal the ire of junior faculty.

Many departments have excellent mathematicians whose excellence is matched by their being a total pain for everyone else. We have all heard of good researchers who sow discord with the same alacrity as they sow good ideas. Remember that the value of a mathematician to a department is not a function of research alone. Maybe your department would be more collegial and have a better research atmosphere if it didn't have to put up with this person's nonsense. If this is the case with Grantsglut, let him/her go. But do a lot of politicking first and talk it over with the dean. There will be repercussions.

As a final case, let's suppose Grantsglut is not such a good researcher or teacher and the university making the offer has a decidedly lower rating than your own. You discuss your opinions with the dean and some of your colleagues and decide to let him/her go. If I were in this situation, I'd just tell Grantsglut that after consulting with the faculty I have decided not to make a counteroffer and I think (s)he should accept the offer. I would not insult him/her — either by word or by making an obviously inadequate response. Don't take this as an opportunity to get something off your chest. Maybe this would make you feel better (maybe!), but you would only be creating an enemy. You will acquire enough enemies in the natural course of events, and there is no need to go out of your way to get another.

I know of two mathematicians who got outside offers that were not countered and who stayed where they were. It was not a pleasant situation. There was bitterness and diminished respect. These faculty clearly used this as a ploy, and their bluff was called. The blame for this situation lies entirely with them and their lack of judgment.

But anyone who does get an external offer must have some good points. A wise head might try to have a long talk with such a colleague, after the dust has settled and the passions cooled. Sure there was an error of judgment, but (s)he remains in your department. There is a misunderstanding of his/her role and value within the department, and this should be addressed. It is doubtful you will ever get this person to see his/her situation as the rest of the department does. But can't you take those virtues that resulted in the outside offer and try to persuade your colleague to forge a career in the department based on these rather than continue as before? This event was traumatic. There may never again be a time when (s)he is as receptive to suggestions about changing.

Day-to-Day Business

§20. Stay active in mathematics.

Easily said. When you become head, everyone wants a piece of you: students, secretaries, faculty, other department heads, deans, registrars, maintenance people. You'll get your fill of being a sought-after commodity, and there will be times when you will long for the anonymity of the professorship. So there will be significant demands on your time. Often it will be impossible for you to sneak off into your private world of scholarship. The times when I find myself most busy are the recruiting season and the closing of tenure and promotion activities, when I must write detailed justifications and politick my colleagues.

Making time for yourself is like saving money. If you don't pursue it consciously, it will never come to be, and you'll wonder how you lost it. My solution is to come into my office, close my door, and not come out until 11:00. My secretary has instructions not to disturb me unless the dean calls or there is an important long-distance call. During the summer I stay home until noon. (I'd stay home until eleven during the academic year except for the parking problem.)

At 11:00 I come out of the office, go through the mail (already presorted by the omniscient Linda), and see what I have to do first. In the afternoon I do my teaching (when I teach) and tend to departmental business. I circulated a memo to the faculty at the beginning of my second year as head telling them this plan, and they have respected my wishes. I got a few comments from some faculty about being a part-time head (I am, in that sense); but if making everyone happy is your ambition, become an airline attendant, not a department head.

Now I have said, "Stay active," not "Keep doing research." Mathematical activity is usually interpreted as research activity, but there are many scholarly things you can do besides research, including working on the curriculum in a significant way.

Why? Personally I enjoy what I do. But the title of this section is an admonition to all department heads. Why do I think this is a good thing? Simply put, it will make your job as department head easier.

Especially if you are the head of a research department, you must maintain the respect of your colleagues. This can be done and has been done by heads who are no longer researchers. But researchers automatically assume that another researcher has certain virtues, while they have to be shown that a non-researcher is not out to make their department into a mediocrity.

There is another reason for a head staying active, but it is not one I can back up with any statistics or scientific evidence. Being deeply involved with the subject tends to harden the wits and hone the reasoning skills. I think this makes for a better decision maker. If you are used to attacking difficult mathematical problems and making sharp distinctions between concepts, deciding a tenure case is easier. Heads who are long and far removed from scholarship tend to want to govern by consensus and committee and to rely less on themselves. Maybe being a successful researcher gives you more confidence and self-reliance.

Another point is that being a researcher myself, I feel I have less difficulty persuading the research mathematicians in my department to do something. For example, we went through calculus reform. The fact that I favored it and had some reputation in research tipped the scales and induced many of my colleagues to approach the subject in a positive way and listen. I am not saying that they automatically went along with what I said. Far from it. But their initial reaction was not skepticism.

I mentioned above that sometimes I do not teach. I did no teaching my first year, but after that I usually taught. It took me a couple of years to realize that I am not superhead. (Several who know me have always thought that is clear.) I enjoy teaching, and after a period of being out of the classroom, I miss it. But a life of administering a department, teaching, doing research, and being a human being is not truly possible, at least not for me. So I will sometimes not teach. As my career as a department head continues, my inclination is to teach less and less. Something has to give, and I have made a personal decision that it will be teaching.

I have also used departmental funds to help me stay active. We have funds available to the faculty to support short-term visitors and I have brought in former students and collaborators who jump start me in some research projects. Having someone to pace me and keep me focused is a good counterweight to the press of administrative duties.

So even though becoming a head is a change in your career, it is not a reason to retire from being an active participant in the development of mathematics.

§21. Making decisions.

One of the most important attributes for a good department head is the ability to make decisions. Decisions must be made not only well but in a timely manner. Indecision is usually worse than a bad decision; it leaves people wondering what is happening, and no one knows where they stand. Also a delay often becomes a decision.

For example, suppose a colleague wants to attend a conference and give a talk. The deadline for submitting an abstract is April 1. If you don't approve the travel before then, you have made a decision that, at the very least, (s)he will not give a talk.

That example is admittedly simplistic; if anything resembling this happens, you have really screwed up. But it exposes the heart of the difficulty with tardy decisions. People are depending on you, and after you act they may have decisions to make, letters to write, abstracts to file, plane reservations to make before the latest discounted fare evaporates, babysitters to find, teaching substitutes to get.

This is not to say that all decisions must or should be made on the same day they arrive on the head's desk, though many can and should. Some require careful deliberation and extensive consultation with colleagues and deans; some will have to await the decision of another administrator in the university. But when all the information is in, you must act. If there is a delay in getting requisite information, all the concerned parties should know it. Deliver the bad news.

A general rule of thumb is that the length of time you take to make a decision should be proportional to the number of people who will be affected by the decision. So a colleague who wants to rent a university automobile to take two students to a nearby colloquium should get an instantaneous decision. (You should already know whether you have the needed funds.) Deciding which calculus book to adopt should take time and get input from the faculty. (If you are wise, you will let a faculty committee make this particular decision.)

One of the crucial decisions is whether to grant tenure (§13). You have to reach a decision here as soon as you can. Delay could be catastrophic.

The art of decision making has several components: (a) deciding who should make the decision, (b) gathering all the pertinent information and consulting with all the relevant principals, (c) taking a stand.

Who should make this decision.

One of the biggest mistakes a head can make is to make all the decisions. Faculty and staff want to exercise control over their lives and feel a sense of accomplishment every bit as much as a head does. In a small operation the head may make almost all the decisions, but this can also be taken to the extreme. Should the head really decide what kind of paper and pens the department buys? This is an important issue (yes it is, folks) but the answer is No!

One guiding principle is to hire good people and then get out of their way while they perform their job. If the department is getting bad paper and pens, point this out to the secretary who orders them. If the problem persists, it means you made a bad decision in who you got to order supplies. It doesn't mean the head should start doing the ordering; it means the head should try to replace the secretary or, at the least, get another secretary to place the orders.

The choice of a text for a course is one best made by the faculty. In fact most non-personnel decisions that will affect the entire department are probably best made by a diverse committee with well-chosen members (see §25), maybe even by the entire faculty. After all, the faculty will be the ones who will have to live with the consequences and carry out and live with this decision. Professors are professionals, not employees. If you exercise too much power in making decisions that affect the way the faculty exercise their profession, they will resent it. Remember that there is a distinction between leadership and tyranny.

Gathering information.

Sometimes gathering information before a decision can be easy, especially if the issue is rather simple. Just ask the faculty and staff their choice of pens. Other times it can be complex. Should the nature of the PhD preliminary exams be changed? Which calculus book should we adopt? Should we hire Professor Derek? For the more complex issues, a committee is a good device for getting information. Several people who take their job seriously and are interested in the outcome can determine the various alternatives and examine their strengths in a way that a single person cannot. Individuals tend to focus quickly on one possible solution, committees almost never restrict themselves to one solution.

I look at the formation of a committee as a process of gathering information and consulting with the rest of the faculty. In my mind this is not a way to make decisions, but in practice it often is. A unanimous committee is a powerful recommendation; one that a wise head will seldom contradict. (See §25.)

Often there is no need for a committee. Information can be suitably gathered by asking a few opinions. I know many frown on this, and such terms as the "ruling clique" are tossed about with scorn by the excluded. Choosing the correct course to follow here will often decide whether you will be remembered as a gifted helmsman or a Captain Bligh*.

But remember that many decisions you will face will have to be made with incomplete information. The ability to make good decisions in such situations will distinguish you.

Taking a stand.

It is undoubtedly the case that no department head in the history of academia has ever had the good fortune to be called upon to decide between 0 and 1. Deciding who to offer a job to is never a choice between competency and incompetency. If the people who come up for tenure are habitually lousy teachers and have never written a paper, you are making bad decisions in a previous sector of your job. If they are always excellent teachers, significant researchers, active committee members, and lovable colleagues, you should write a book.

When the decision is yours to make and you have as much information as you are ever going to get, it is time to act and act without delay. If it is a tough one, take a walk, set a deadline for reaching the decision, talk with a trusted advisor (a colleague, your spouse, the dean). Then take a stand and know why you have reached that decision. Be prepared to defend it.

So that last decision you made was a mistake. What should you do? Certainly you should admit it to yourself. Whether you should admit your mistake to others depends on circumstances. Despite the announced emphasis in academia on substance, perception and appearance are influential. It is important for your colleagues to have

---

* A person who has been unjustly maligned by popular movies based on the tale of a scurrilous dog. See *Bligh* by Gavin Kennedy.

confidence in you. There will be some things you will have to stand up and take the blame for. In such a situation I would advocate doing it soon, before someone else points a finger, and advertising what you are going to do to correct the mistake, make amends, or prevent its recurrence. If you start worrying what your colleagues will think of you, you are exacerbating the problem. (Are you listening, Washington?)

But there is no need to advertise your lapses. For example, suppose you missed the deadline for nominating Professor Artofall for a teaching award. Should you put out a memo telling everyone? No. Should you tell Professor Artofall? Maybe. But it might be better to just nominate her next time.

To the extent you can, correct your mistakes. Call the dean and ask if the teaching awards committee has met and can you get Professor Artofall's nomination in this afternoon.

If you have a large number of lapses, missed deadlines, tardy appointments, maybe you should examine yourself and your organization. A good secretary will help you avoid these.

In my academic career I have been a director of undergraduates and a director of graduate students for a mathematics department. I believed then that there was no mistake I could make that I could not correct. This may have been a consequence of my perpetual optimism, but I still believe it was true. I do not believe it applies to my present position as head.

If you recommend to the dean that an assistant professor be terminated, it is irreversible. If you discover that recommendation was a mistake (this really should never happen), you better keep it to yourself. Yes, you do put a blotch on someone's career and cause them pain and suffering. But there is a larger issue here. If you try reversing your recommendation, you will destroy your credibility with the dean, and this will have adverse consequences in the future for the entire department. It is quite likely that even reversing yourself on such an issue will have no affect on the final disposition of this case. But the consequences for the future will be dramatic and unmistakable.

If there is a mistake you have made that is so horrific that you cannot live with it and must reverse yourself even though it will cause irreparable harm to the department, you should probably fall on the sword and resign as head.

When should you take a vote, and when should you act on your own?

A tricky question without a clear answer. Answering this question, nevertheless, will determine a major part of your success as head. Even in a department such as mine, where there is a stated university policy that all votes are advisory to the head and where the faculty state their agreement with this policy, it is often essential that there be a vote. And countermanding a majority vote even under these circumstances is an adventure not embarked on lightly.

But the question here is whether you should even take a vote. Mathematics departments are not democracies — at least, they should not be. Some people's opinions should be weighted more than others. This violates the basic emotions of most American faculty. Nevertheless, a process of talking to your colleagues, deciding whether the opposition or support for a particular measure is deeply felt or superficial, figuring whether the faculty who will be affected the most are in the pro or con column, and then deciding on your own is often a wiser course than taking a vote.

As a head, you may want to have a vote only when you know what the outcome will be. Certainty is a sweet emotion. But some issues are too critical to avoid a vote. I also find it difficult to know how a vote will turn out. I've been dramatically wrong on several occasions. Before I was head, I had a rather good track record of predicting votes. As head the faculty are often unwilling to confide in me, especially if they believe their view is contrary to mine. So don't bank on your predictions.

The only practical guideline I can think of is to vote on issues that will affect everyone, and don't vote on others. This won't always be applicable. Recruiting affects all, but most times if you had a vote to decide what area to recruit in, the votes would be scattered. It is probably more factious to have a vote on this issue than for you to have a lot of discussion and then decide.

We were recently forced to go through a process of eliminating some journal subscriptions. This affected everyone, but a vote would have been absurd; everyone would have voted to eliminate journals in areas other than their own. So we had *lots* of discussions and several trial lists were circulated for comments and objections. In the end I was the one that recommended the cuts to the library.

By the way, don't always avoid a vote just because there is no

hope of a majority for one side of an issue. This phenomenon can
work in your favor. If the opinions are fractured, the issue is not too
serious, and there is not a lot of passion involved, you can do what
you want. I'd be reluctant, however, to plunge into a major course
change without significant backing from the faculty. For some issues
you will need a clear mandate.

§22. Lean years and plush years.

Anyone can be a good head when the times are plush. It takes a
real pro to do the job right when the times are lean. Also the
plush years are few and far between. Over time, lean is the dominant
theme.

Actually, I've never had a plush year. Perhaps the nature of
the national downsizing, the global economy, the saturation of the
national job market with college graduates means that universities
will not see the plush years of the past. As a faculty member, the
only years that I ever saw that were truly well funded were in the
late sixties. There were enormous numbers of PhDs being produced
as a consequence of Sputnik, and mathematics departments expanded
to find places for them. The size of some mathematics departments
tripled.

So don't count on getting a windfall. Set your agenda for times
of constant or slowly increasing budgets. Should there be a budget
boon, this will prepare you for a response, and you will, no doubt,
have many worthy places where you can spend the bonanza.

In November of my first year as head (1990), the university announced a 2% cutback in the current budget. That is, the university
had to return 2% of its current budget to the state. Since the budgets of academic departments are mostly salaries, I didn't have to
return 2% of my budget, but I was given a dollar amount to return,
and it was painful. It devastated the travel budget, eliminated paper
graders, and drastically cut into our use of supplies. I was calling for
conservation of paper and the elimination of long distance. Then I
was told that, by July 1, one secretary and all continuing part-time
faculty had to be dismissed. The economy was bad, and the state had
informed the university that it should expect additional cuts in the
next budget.

I was depressed about this and wondered what I had gotten into.
My doubts were quelled when I heard that just about every other

university was going through similar contortions. Being a supreme optimist, I tried to find some good in the situation, but my optimism was severely taxed. But because it was the beginning of my headship, my honeymoon period, the faculty were very understanding and cooperative. Many were downright sympathetic with my being faced with such a welcome.

I have already described how my secretary found another position, so that part of the crisis passed with no pain. We had only one part-time faculty member who had to leave, and he took an early retirement. The worst aspect of the budget crisis was cutting back on the operating budget and not having paper graders. In my mind, paper graders in mathematics are an integral part of instruction. With large classes (when it comes to grading papers, even a class of 30 students is large), having assistance in grading makes a difference in how much homework is assigned. We all recognize that doing mathematics is the best way to learn mathematics. Most students do not have the discipline to work lots of problems on their own initiative. If a professor has a paper grader, it is more likely that homework will be assigned and collected on a regular basis. (Many will take that as a criticism of mathematics professors. Perhaps it is. Like a lot of issues, you can rail against life because it isn't the way it ought to be or you can deal with reality.)

In the final analysis, some good did come from all this. Borrowing a term from the business world, we restructured. All aspects of the department's operation were closely examined, some were eliminated, and those that weren't were streamlined.

One fact that was helpful in a lean year was the lack of restrictions by my university on how I shifted money in the department's budget. I get the impression that Tennessee is in the minority here. I have the ability to shift money earmarked for telephones to paper, for example. If a GTA resigns after a semester, it is possible for me to use that salary for the phone bill, as long as I meet the teaching responsibilities. In a time of crisis, this is a balm. I have the impression that this is not the case at most universities. Requiring department heads to keep the money in the original piles strikes me as a form of micromanagement.

So what's my advice during lean times? To begin with, don't bellyache. You're not the only department head in your college who has problems. The dean has a large share of this as well. If there is a time in your career to be a team player, this is it. This doesn't mean you have to spread your optimistic outlook to the college; in fact, it's probably best to keep this in the department. But help the college to work through the difficulties. After the crisis is over, you can diplomatically remind the dean how cooperative you were.

If budgets are essentially constant, money for a new project has to be created by eliminating some other activity. Whatever is added here must be subtracted from somewhere — either in the college or elsewhere in the university. Remember this when you present your plans to the dean. This doesn't mean you should hold back when making a proposal. It is your job to make plans that will improve the research, teaching, and service mission of the mathematics department. It is the dean's job to decide whether improving mathematics is more important than improving Arabic studies. It is the chancellor's job to decide whether giving money to the College of Arts and Sciences for improving mathematics is more important than expanding the accounting program.

Whatever you do, don't try to tell the dean what other department should be cut to fund mathematics. Just be positive. Present your proposal. Justify it. Outline the benefits. Don't knock another program. Doing this will create a negative impression of you and the department. Sure you think recruiting Professor Aufschloss is the greatest opportunity the university has seen since its founding. But the art department thinks that keeping Pisto, its artist in residence and the candidate for the chief artist at the Malibu Art Institute, is far more important. Unless the campus administration can be persuaded to fund both, the dean will have to choose. Or do neither. I think talking against art is unwise. Talk in favor of mathematics.

§23. Perseverance.

Never stop trying. Don't ever expect that a proposal that you make to your college will ever bring instant acceptance and funding. Celebrate if it does, but don't ever expect it. Nevertheless keep at it. Make sure your proposal is sound, has definite goals that are achievable, and, if successful, benefits more than just your own department. Be sure that the funding you are requesting is needed for the project and will be used to achieve the stated goals.

Don't ever underestimate the administration. They are not stupid. If they detect a phony argument or think you are trying to put one over on them, they will react just like you would if you were in their place, and you and your department will suffer — as you should.

For example, suppose you draw up a request for additional faculty to decrease class size in finite mathematics. At least that's what you tell the dean. What you really want is to get additional researchers. You can bet (s)he will ask why it takes a PhD to teach such a course and why can't instructors be used. Do you really think the dean won't be aware that the people you bring in will not be teaching only finite mathematics?

If you keep making a proposal and it is continually rejected, ask yourself why. Ask the dean why. Doesn't this proposal go toward meeting his/her goals as well as yours? Maybe the rejections are due to skepticism about you and your department's willingness or ability to carry out your plan. One underlying theme here is that you and your dean have to share a lot of things, including mutual respect and confidence in one another.

The principal theme of this section is that if you are proposing something that will benefit mathematics and the rest of the college, if your proposal is sound, and if you have the confidence of the dean, don't ever stop just because you are told no. Why should you? If this is truly a meritorious proposition, one that you feel essential for the development of the department that is in your vision, then don't abandon it. It's worth fighting for, so fight.

Remember that unless new money is entering the university, not just money to keep pace with inflation, the dean will have to convince the administration to give the college resources that are currently in another unit. Or the dean will have to demolish another department, an event (s)he may find harder to justify. What you have to strive for with your dean is making your number-one priority his/her number-one priority. If you politick well, with persistence and prudence, the merits of the case will eventually prevail.

§24. Paperwork.

A lot of non-heads fear this and talk about it as an impediment to ever taking the job. For me it is the easiest part of being a head. I just do it. I am also better at it now than when I began. (There is something to be said for on-the-job training.) I have always enjoyed working with words, and this is a desirable trait for being a head. It isn't essential, just desirable, and it helps in dispatching paper.

It isn't that the paperwork is not important, though much of it is not. The trivial stuff can be handled as if you were working on an assembly line. The important matters better be treated like working on a research proposal.

Mail comes in every day and with it an assortment of junk, near junk, the slightly important, and the critical. The junk is my favorite type of mail because it is the easiest to process. My classification of junk has remained constant since my pre-head days.

My secretary opens and sorts the mail. Many things addressed to me never come before my eyes, as she redirects it to a more appropriate person. As head of the department, you are identified by everyone in the university and beyond as its representative. You are the one they send mail to and ask for on the phone. In a large department like mine, there are several people whose job it is to handle certain tasks that outsiders might think belong to the head. But no outsider knows this. It helps to have a secretary who knows who should answer the query of the moment. When there is a doubt about some piece of mail, I get it. At this point I might direct the mail to someone else. Often I ask one of the associate heads or my administrative assistant to handle it.

As a head you do get some additional mail. There seem to be a lot of questionnaires. As I did before becoming head, I throw most of these away. I don't see why I should spend my time making someone else's job easier when I don't even know this person. Some surveys, however, are important. There are the various AMS and MAA surveys. I have great loyalty to the profession, but these are the kinds of things my secretary and administrative assistant can do far more efficiently than I. I am also asked to fill out forms evaluating various administrators; I do this religiously.

It is said that you should conduct your business so that you only touch each piece of paper once. I don't know who first said this; there are many whom I have heard given credit. It's a goal, but like many goals, I can't always meet it. I keep my dictaphone handy while going through my mail. Sometimes my secretary can write a letter following my general directions; she has a whole collection of old letters on the computer. But I regularly get things I either cannot or do not want to handle at the moment. I need someone's advice, and they are out of town or are busy. Maybe I am busy writing an article or collaborating with a visitor, and I just don't want to be interrupted.

I mentioned I use a dictaphone. I suggest you do too. Letters and reports that are dictated are not as elegant as those I sit down and write. But they get out quicker. Really strange sentence constructions can be changed when you proofread the typed version. But if you insist on writing every letter and report, be prepared to spend a lot of time at it. That's time you would be better off spending elsewhere — like reading the *Monthly* or *Mathematical Intelligencer* or working in your garden.

Another use of the dictaphone arises after meetings with my colleagues. If the meeting was important, I dictate a memo to the colleague, with a copy to the files, about what happened. I really should say that I try to do this. I forget or neglect this, and I often suffer the consequences. Such a record on paper, or in electronic form, reminds us both what was agreed to: how much travel money I committed, when the leave is to take place, which semester they are to have a reduced teaching load, and what they have to do for this. Sending out copies of such memos is also a convenient way for me to notify whoever needs to know about the commitment: the bookkeeper, the administrative assistant, the scheduling officer, one of the associate heads.

Then there is the really critical stuff: budget requests, tenure and promotion documents, letters of recommendation. If I were a faculty member, I would want my head to treat these with great care. I follow my own advice here; such matters get my complete devotion. I treat the reports I write for the budget and tenure and promotion cases as though I was writing a paper on which my own tenure rested. Otherwise I would be laying the groundwork for disaster.

If the faculty think that the important matters are not getting your full attention, they will see you as not living up to your responsibilities. You are there to lead them. They trusted you, you got a pay raise to do this job, you asked for the position, and now this is the way you respond. What a mistake they made! If you cannot put your best efforts into the projects that are essential for the advancement of the department, then you are not leading.

If the dean ascertains that you are being perfunctory in these matters, you will be perceived as weak and ineffective. Your proposals and judgments will not be given due consideration. If you want to be successful, this is one place where you must spend some time. You won't always get what you want, but in the long run a conscientious effort on these important matters will bear fruit. After you get into this, you will see that it is a form of scholarship. Do this well. You will have a clear conscience that you have done your best and fulfilled your contract with your colleagues.

Then there is email. As a faculty member I loved email. When I have organized a conference, I have made nightly offerings to the gods of etherworld. But as a department head I have mixed emotions about it.

Email still offers me all the advantages it did in my pre-head days, more so since more people use it now. But it also increases my accessibility. I think I am asked things through email I wouldn't be asked otherwise. Often, I believe, a question pops into a colleague's mind and (s)he sends me an email message. Without this outlet those questions might have faded into irrelevance, been answered without any special effort on my part, or perhaps been answered at the afternoon tea or during a stroll down the hall. But a question asked demands an answer, and I type slowly.

I really haven't figured out how to handle email as efficiently as other things I do. I keep trying. Sometimes I dictate a response and my secretary does the typing. Other times I just forward her the message without comment and she figures out what to do. (Another blessing of having a good secretary.) But many of the tasks my secretary does in the handling of regular mail are carried out by me for email. That's not good, but I don't know what else to do.

Email and departmental networks are still rather new, and I keep finding new ways to use them. In meetings of the major committees a secretary takes the minutes, and these are circulated to the entire faculty. This improves the general knowledge about what is happening in the department. The minutes of the Undergraduate Committee are also sent to the neighboring community colleges, since what we do affects their programs. Occasionally minutes of the committees are sent to other departments in the university. The department maintains various distribution lists on its network for all the committees as well as various subsets of the faculty (full professors, instructors, tenured faculty, etc.).

Most of these things could be accomplished without email, but it is easier to do with it. In fact, things like this were not done before the arrival of the department network. Sometimes it's too easy to distribute email mesages to a large audience. We've had a couple of occasions when arguments between faculty were played out via the Internet with copies to the entire faculty. But who can say that this is all bad? Perhaps getting gripes out in the open facilitates resolution.

My advice to those who are irritated is to put away for 24 hours any letter written in anger. (I have sometimes failed, to my regret, to heed my own advice.) With email it is harder to follow this sagacious course.

In sum I am happy that email exists. I like the age of electronics. In fact I find myself more capable of filing and keeping track of electronic documents and messages than those on paper. If I can just figure out how to keep from spending so much time at the keyboard.

§25. How to form a committee.

Forming a committee can be tricky. Exactly how the committee is constituted and how much care you should apply to forming it depends on the importance of the work. Standing committees, like the Undergraduate Committee or the Graduate Committee, need balance and broad representation. If the decisions of a committee are going to be respected by the rest of the faculty, you should be sure that you have not packed the committee with people representing your point of view. Talk with your associate heads about the appointments. Appoint a chair for the committee and consult with this chair about the membership.

When I say that committees should be balanced, I am not necessarily referring to their field of expertise, but rather their viewpoints. Certain kinds of committees need to have members with a particular research background. If there is an Applied Mathematics Committee, you should be sure that at least some members are applied. But I have never seen the need to have every area of mathematics represented on the Undergraduate Committee. To be sure, if that committee will consider a new computational requirement for the bachelor degree, you should appoint some members with the required expertise. If you start trying to balance committees by areas, you are injecting a political element into what should be an intellectual enterprise.

Calculus reform is a hot topic these days. Suppose you invent the Calculus Committee to make a recommendation to the department on which of the several reform materials will be adopted. Now this is an issue that will heat the blood. Passions will be apparent. If you load the committee with the department's most avid reformers, you can bet that the conservative faculty will never listen to their recommendations. Try to achieve an equipoise of points of view.

Inevitably committees are divided into active and passive participants. There are usually very few active members, sometimes maybe only one. Invariably there is at least one. These are the folks who seem to have a passion for the business at hand and have strong opinions on what direction should be taken. The rest of the members are somewhat passive. They agreed to serve on the committee because its part of their job. They think that the business at hand is important if for no other reason than because everything associated with the academic enterprise is. But they have no strong opinions on these matters. They expect to attend the meetings, become informed, and make an enlightened judgment.

In my career I have been an active as well as a passive member of various committees. The active members often give a committee its initial direction. Often they define the issues. If all the members were active, there would be gridlock and nothing would come out of the committee. If all were passive, inertia would be the consuming mood and nothing would come out of the committee. Keep this in mind when you make appointments.

If you appoint to the Graduate Committee Professor Puccini, who for the past three years has been advocating that all PhD candidates pass an exam in advanced calculus before being allowed to take the usual battery of prelims, be confident that this issue will be on the agenda of the committee. For matters involving the graduate program there is usually much passion, and you probably don't have to worry excessively about balancing Professor Puccini's view. This is an issue that just about every committee member will have an opinion on.

But what about your appointment to the same committee of Professor Internerd, who believes all PhD candidates should have a mastery of at least one computer language? This is probably an issue that most of us are undecided about. It certainly was not part of our graduate education. It has merits. Are there drawbacks? This is a case when you might want to make an effort to balance Professor Internerd with another appointment to the committee. Maybe appoint Professor Firmbase, who thinks doctoral candidates should learn what he learned while in graduate school. Maybe it's better to just appoint Professor Triedtrue, whose steady, calm approach to all problems always seems to get to the bottom of things and who enjoys wide respect in the faculty.

Should students be on a committee?

Having students on a committee is a practice that isn't universal but exists in many places. This strikes me as a holdover from the sixties. I have basic philosophical objections to students being on most departmental committees. Certainly if students are going to be asked to carry out the decisions of the committee, I would include them in the membership. Planning the department picnic, picking the annual math day speaker, making teaching awards all seem appropriate places for student input. But committees that will discuss changing the curriculum? Set degree requirements? I don't think students should be involved here.

The proponents of Total Quality Management (TQM, in their sinister lexicon) who inhabit the halls of academia advocate considering the "student as customer". Baloney! Customers know what they want. Students know they want an education or a degree (not the same thing, as most faculty but few students know). But they really don't know what this is all about.

Besides, who says we should consider students as customers? Why not consider them as our product? Our raw material? Either viewpoint would radically alter the discussion. I fully believe that thinking of the students as customers is entirely proper for the treasurer's office, the halls of residence, and the food service. But if the faculty ever stumble down that path, the precipice is not far away.

Students also have very short memories and always tend to want to make policy based on their experience with their latest difficulty. They also have a conflict of interest. Even if whatever program changes will affect only students who follow those on the committee, there is a built-in conflict of interest. My advice is to keep them off these committees and find another way to get them involved.

§26. Dealing with budgets.

Planning and administering a budget is another of those topics that seem to cause heads-in-waiting concern. It's really a lot less trouble than you might think, but here is another place where having an administrative assistant helps.

In our office we have two people who deal regularly with budget matters: the administrative assistant and a bookkeeper. The bookkeeper handles most of the day-to-day money problems such as filing for travel reimbursements, pay forms for various employees, paying the invoice for office supplies, etc. The administrative assistant oversees this work and keeps track of the overall budget as well as creates the budgets for any grant proposals.

As soon as I became head, I asked for a simple budget layout. Give me a spreadsheet printout with columns indicating what we are given for the various categories (faculty, GTA, and staff salaries; phone; xeroxing; etc.) and any recoveries we anticipate (income from a grant, for example, or salary that is released by a colleague who is going on an unpaid leave). Also have columns for what we have already spent, what is encumbered, what we anticipate spending, and so on. Then have the balance. This way I can see where the money is coming from, where it's going, and what freedom and flexibility I have. This seemed pretty straightforward to me, though my first administrative assistant thought it an unusual and strange approach. (She left the job after a year and returned to school to get an MBA.) The next administrative assistant thought it a natural request.

At first I would get updates on this every month, but now we go two or three months between updates. It helps me and my administrative assistant to see where there might be difficulties and whether we have some flexibility. I mentioned before that I have a lot of flexibility to shift money from one category to another (§22). As the fiscal year draws to a close, this spreadsheet analysis shows me if I have some funds that look as though they might not get spent. At my university I cannot carry money forward from one fiscal year to the next. So at this point I try to see if there is some computing machinery we need (we always do) and I decide what to buy. If there is a tidy sum available, I might offer to pay a colleague a summer stipend to complete a specific project. In the past I have gotten manuals written for using graphing calculators, had statistics compiled for the placement exam, and had a collection of calculus-computer exercises manufactured.

The dean is also looking for additional money sources near the end of the fiscal year and will often ask department heads to return some money if they have any available. I believe my dean has rather good information about the status of my budget, and, if I have a healthy surplus in May, might ask me to return a specific amount. When such a call comes, I try to respond. I don't go near the edge of being insolvent — far from it. But this is another of those points where some trust and cooperation might be rewarded in the future. You can count on there being a year when you will have to go to the dean and announce that your operating budget is about to blush. In return for a bailout of you or in anticipation of it, giving back a few thousand dollars might be a good investment.

There is also the planning for next year's budget. Some of this is a "wish list". This is the time when I promulgate the department's plans. I approach this in a direct way. I simply say what I would like to see happen and what I think it will cost. There is little mystery here. It is my job to propose a plan for improving the research and teaching mission of the Mathematics Department. The dean will make a decision to support me and look for the required resources, or (s)he won't. As I have said elsewhere, I do this in a realistic way. There is no point in giving the impression that I am unaware of the dean's budget problems, and I never ask for anything without complete justification.

When determining the cost of a project, an additional brain or two thinking about this is helpful. Be realistic but don't overlook anything (you probably will). If the project is really expensive, see if you can spread it out over more than one year. There is little point in asking money for next year that won't be used until later. The dean and his/her assistants will likely discover such mistakes, and this will diminish their confidence in your figures.

We have to prioritize our requests, but I'd do this even if I wasn't required to do so. Recent years have seen tight budgets, and what I have asked for has been about 2 to 3 percent of my present budget plus whatever raises I am seeking. The fiscal conditions would have to have veered toward fantasy land for me ever to ask for more than 5%.

§27. Meetings with the dean.

Whenever I have a meeting with the dean, I prepare. If I have a request to make, I write a memo that I bring to the meeting. This memo states what I am asking in clear terms. If there is more than one request, I write a separate memo for each request. This puts in front of his eyes a clearly stated proposal. In the course of our conversation, I can amplify and clarify any points that are not understood.

With this memo I and the dean have a record of what the meeting was about. If he agrees to my request, then I ask him to initial an approval on the memo and make a copy for my file. Often what is approved is a modification of what I proposed, and it is necessary, in light of our conversation, for me to rewrite the memo. Later I send a copy of the modified memo for initialling. Some important things take place in these meetings, and the last thing you want is that you and your dean do not have a clear understanding of what happened.

§28. Relations with other departments.

Many mathematics departments have a long tradition of close relations with the physics department. Good. But mathematics departments must begin to broaden their contacts within the university, to say nothing of society. All the sciences — physical, biological, and social — have begun to use more mathematics and their students are almost certainly enrolled in a variety of mathematics courses. We also have a unique and important service role in the university. No other department has as many non-majors enrolled in its senior level courses as mathematics. To the extent that research contacts are possible, all the better. But a department head has a limited role in the creation of research collaboration. The department head can nurture a research interest that exists, but (s)he can do little to create a collaboration.

A well-run mathematics department will never lose sight of its service roll. If it does, it imperils all its remaining missions. A consideration of what happened at the University of Rochester, where the university administration recommended the elimination of the PhD program in mathematics, is a good case in point. (This recommendation was later withdrawn.) Part of the difficulties at Rochester seem to stem from their neglect of other departments. When the American Mathematical Society took the stance, supported by other science groups as well as the Rochester mathematics department, that a good graduate program in mathematics is essential for good graduate programs in the sciences, the university administration seemed to counter with, "If so, why hasn't our mathematics department paid more attention to its service roll?" The Rochester mathematics department also seemed to lack allies within the university in its efforts to keep the PhD program afloat.

In these times of economic flux, no department head should ever feel that anything is permanent. Deans have the right, the obligation, to eliminate programs they feel are not contributing to the university's mission. If a university's income is constant and its expenses are increasing, something has to give. In such a situation, deans and presidents must cut expenses. This means they must either eliminate programs or diminish the quality of all programs across the board. They simply cannot run a deficit.

In the case of Rochester I was neither a witness, nor have I spoken to people who were. So my opinions should be judged in that light.

Everyone, however, feels that a number of mistakes were made. Many in the mathematics community faulted the university administration. The lack of an external review committee, for example, has been cited as well as their use of the ratings of mathematics departments by the National Research Council and *U.S. News and World Report*. The use of *U.S. News and World Report* initially struck me as bizarre and the ratings by the National Research Council somewhat more defensible. After some thought I began to wonder if the opposite judgment may have more validity.

The National Research Council ratings have a patina of intellectualism about them, but it is a grossly unscientific exercise. Deans suggest to the NRC faculty from their departments to make the ratings. These faculty are then sent a list of 50 departments in their discipline, with a list of all the faculty in those departments, and asked for their ratings. My first criticism is the choice of the raters. What does a dean know? They know what others say and the size of research contracts. In mathematics this probably skews the ratings in favor of those departments which have heavy representation in areas where funding is more generous. In the physical and biological sciences, unfunded research is seldom good research. Big bucks are needed for all those labs. In mathematics nothing could be further from the truth. The top ten mathematics departments on the NRC list are probably on everyone's list (± 1). Beyond that it's a crap shoot. But if you build it, they will come. Information generated by such a prestigious organization as the NRC is going to be used.

From the standpoint of a large state university, the use of *U.S. News and World Report* as a means of judgment would truly be ludicrous. In the case of a university that depends heavily on tuition income, like Rochester, and whose mission is heavily focused on undergraduate education, it is less so. Which university a student chooses is so dependent on perception. Yes, there may be the advice of a high school counselor. But that advice also depends on perception. *U.S. News and World Report* is a measure of that perception, and so the use of this popular, non-academic expression of opinion may be even more valid in Rochester's decision-making process than the report of the NRC.

As for not having an external review of the department, I wonder how valuable this would have been. The PhD program at Rochester is good. They have creditable faculty. There are many PhD programs in the country that are way below the one at Rochester. (On the other hand if you stay within a 400-mile radius of Rochester their relative position probably decreases.) In these circumstances, I doubt that any team of mathematicians would have furnished the university administration with the kind of information they needed. They may have fared just as well flying by the seat of their administrative pants.

I think the greatest mistake made was the university administration's decision to have calculus taught by non-mathematicians and adjunct faculty. That will seriously diminish the quality of instruction in a course that is a cornerstone of undergraduate education. It seems to me that they made a decision that contradicts their primary mission. But maybe the importance of calculus instruction was never made clear to them, either in words or in deeds. No one, not even the team sent by the American Mathematical Society to look at what was happening at Rochester, has ever said how the mathematics department there taught calculus. Large classes? Unsupervised graduate students? Courses untailored to the needs of the scientists and engineers? I don't know what the situation was, but I know what should be avoided.

A department head should convince the faculty that service courses are their life's blood. The graduate program and the undergraduate major program are our soul, but service pays the bills. You just cannot ignore them or treat them like the inconvenience that so many mathematicians do. And part of performing this service is making sure that the client departments are getting what they want. Essential to all this is finding out what they want, and this can only be done by talking to them.

We recently went through a two-year exercise in calculus reform. One of the real benefits was extensive discussions with our engineering and science faculties. This produced several dramatic surprises. Some of our faculty said things like, "I know we really don't like so much emphasis on computation, but it's important to the engineers." In fact the engineers told us to please emphasize concepts, interpretation of graphs, growth rates. Hey folks, this is what mathematicians like to teach. When we discussed an undergraduate course combining linear algebra and differential equations, the engineers were more enthusiastic than our undergraduate committee.

In connection with calculus reform we had several outside speakers, discussion panels, and faculty meetings. The engineers and science faculty were invited to them all. In the end we embraced calculus reform, and we also cemented relations with the College of Engineering and the various science departments in the College of Arts & Sciences.

Similar things happened when we revised a two-semester sequence in polynomial calculus and finite mathematics. In addition to getting a better sequence, we had increased contact with the social sciences and our College of Business. Curriculum reform is a dynamic process that must be continual, but it should never take place in a vacuum. In fact, it's a splendid opportunity to make contact with your colleagues outside the department.

Interdisciplinary programs seem very fashionable today. There certainly is a lot of funding for them. It's an attractive undertaking if it's done right, and the product can be a program that is highly attractive and, perhaps, unique. It could also be a sham. Money has a way of attracting the academic lowlife from under their rock of deserved obscurity. I have seen great expenditures to establish programs that few students ever pursue. But there is sometimes wheat amongst that chaff.

The essential ingredient here is to be sure you have faculty who, besides being academically astute, are intellectually committed to an interdisciplinary program. Mathematics is so extensively used that such joint ventures are natural for it. The use of mathematics as an organizing, unifying, and predicting tool is clear to us and to many scientists. But realize that many in the science departments have limited mathematical background. They need to be educated and so do you. Even if no interdisciplinary program results, the discussions themselves may be worth the time spent.

The colloquium is, of course, another avenue of interdepartmental dialogue. Use it. Invite someone from another department to address the mathematics department and explain how they use mathematics. The mathematics may be unsophisticated. So what. Your faculty and students will understand more than they would if the talk was by a visiting mathematician on last month's research results. Perhaps you might designate some of your mathematical colleagues to be the official questioners, people who can ask questions without reserve whenever any scientific point arises they believe will be obscure to the rest of the audience.

The important point is to open lines of communication. Joint ventures will follow. Besides, isn't this an attraction of academic life? When I got my PhD, I thought I had a future of great discussions with experts on a variety of my scientific, literary, and historical interests.

One of my early disappointments was the lack of contact with faculty outside mathematics. Only when I became a department head did I begin to meet non-mathematics faculty with the kind of frequency I had anticipated as a graduate student.

§29. Dress.

I confess. I like to wear good clothes. For me, putting on a tie and a sport coat is not a chore. In fact, wearing a comfortable shirt, a good tie and coat, or a sweater and coat, gives me pleasure.

You may or may not enjoy wearing good clothes, but I think department heads should dress somewhat better than they did before assuming the job. Quit snickering and listen to what I have to say.

The summer before I assumed my duties as head, I had a conversation with the administrative assistant at my former university, who gave me several pieces of advice. One thing she said, as I sat there in shorts and sandals, was that I should dress better than I was. She said that as a head I should never come to the office in shorts.

Non-academics put a lot of emphasis on appearance. Academics do also, but the parameters are different. The vast majority of Americans tend to judge you and react to you based as much on the way you look and act as on what you say and believe. If you are dubious, just go back to the first appearance of President Jimmy Carter on television in a sweater and remember the kind of reaction it elicited. When, as an energy-saving step, the US House of Representatives raised the summer thermostat, one of its members showed up in tie but without a jacket. The Speaker of the House, the late Tip O'Neil, publicly ordered him to leave the floor.

There is a strong public sentiment that the way you dress indicates the extent of your respect for what is going on. Your faculty colleagues may not get upset. In fact, faculty generally do not react to clothing. But I can guarantee you that others will if you are too casual about what you wear. This includes the staff, parents, deans, and, believe it or not, students.

When I interview people for a job, I can be adversely affected by what they wear. I don't recall ever refusing to hire anyone because they were sloppily dressed; certainly a casual dresser has never upset me. But there have been folks I have interviewed who were wearing what seemed to be dirty clothes, and I got a very negative impression. If someone comes for an interview, I expect they are putting their best foot forward. I assume they understand this is serious business, and in my mind the way they dress reflects how serious they are.

Wearing jeans, t-shirt, and the same shoes you wear for your noontime run is making a dramatic statement of how you want to be regarded. The same is true of wearing a coat and tie, but to a far lesser degree.

In essence, wearing a coat and tie is a neutral act. When you wear a tie, it is normal and customary behavior that means nothing (unless you are wearing it to a barbeque). At best, it means I am serious and I want you to regard me that way. If you show up for class or a meeting with frayed shorts and a t-shirt, you are saying I am free and easy and nothing really matters to me. Wear what you want in the privacy of your home, but if you want to gain the attention of the public – and, as head, you need to do this – dress the part of the head.

§30. Socializing.

There is a part of your life as head that is social. Schools differ dramatically in their social life. My impression is that the number of departmental parties is inversely proportional to the population of the ambient city. Which is preferable depends on your tastes. My advice, like most people's, is the result of my own experiences. Do what you want to. Don't feel you *have* to entertain.

I do go to dinner with some visitors to the department. Sometimes I have a visitor over to my home after their talk, and we open a bottle of champagne before going out to dinner. Then, of course, there is the entertaining of job candidates. What I do depends on the number of positions we are trying to fill in the given year. In our way of doing things, there is a lunch and a dinner associated with each interview. One year we had 14 candidates in during a three-week period. I just cannot take that much food, and I limited myself to one meal per candidate. I still gained a couple of pounds.

There is another type of socializing that I think of as somewhat more important: going to lunch with your colleagues. It's a good way to keep your ear to the departmental ground. You can also launch a few trial balloons at lunch and get initial reactions to some projects. The ideal would be to lunch with different groups, but that never seems to work out.

The one head I knew personally who was thrown out of office never went to lunch with his colleagues. I am not implying a cause-and-effect relationship, but if he had talked with his colleagues more (which did not have to be done over lunch), he might have sensed the growing dissatisfaction with the way he was running things. I cannot conceive of a head weathering a storm of discontent by battening down the hatches and isolating himself/herself from the controversy.

Another head who was elected to his position told me that, when he was selected, the department's choice came down to him and one other professor. He is convinced that he won because his competition always had lunch with the same group of five faculty, who were perceived as a "ruling clique". I have no idea whether this is true or not. It is, however, a comment on the power of perception.

When Should You Quit?

For some this is not a question that needs to be addressed. A fixed term of office will make this one less decision to make. Others might be thrown out either by the faculty or the dean. So the first piece of advice on this topic is not to let this happen. Quit before you are even close to being ejected. It may be that a movement to forcibly remove the head from office has not begun. But if there are symptoms of this, go while you can do so with dignity and the respect of your colleagues.

I am not alone in having observed department heads who have held onto office too long — those who have remained in the chair until they were the sole faculty member who thought their position was still tenable. Such heads become estranged from the faculty and just cannot resume their position as a colleague in the department. The only solution at this point is a job at another university or another administrative post in their current institution. Ending their term of office on such a note makes either of these a difficult maneuver.

One friend said that his experience as a head was that he acquired one enemy per year. I've known those who have acquired enemies at a far greater speed, but this seems fairly accurate. You may do better; perhaps you are a saint, the head of a small department with no conflicts, or are not making the hard decisions. (In this last case, you'll probably go for a long time making no enemies, and then the entire department will turn against you in an avalanche of irritation over nothing getting done.)

In any case, this might be used to figure an upper bound for how long to stay in office. Divide the size of the faculty by 3, and figure you should probably not hang around much longer than that number of years. If more than a third of the faculty consider themselves enemies or are considered by you as your enemy, it's probably time to return to the ranks.

I think that it might be a good idea to get away from the job occasionally. In fact, a sabbatical is as good an idea for a head as for any other faculty. It might also be good for the rest of the department so they can appreciate what a splendid job you do by seeing what trouble pops up while you are away. If you do take a leave, you should get away from campus. Leave town. Otherwise your replacement will find it too easy to consult with you, and you will be besieged with phone calls from across campus by people who do not know you are on leave.

It's important that when you take a leave you choose an appropriate person as an acting head. Some might think, especially in light of my comment about a leave making people realize what a great head you are, that I mean your replacement should be someone doomed to failure. You certainly don't want that. Besides, a really bad temporary head will make your job all the more difficult upon your return. It might also artificially increase your list of enemies by one very bitter ex-acting head. Your acting head might be an associate head. It might be anyone on the faculty who is organized and respected by your colleagues. Since the term is short and fixed, it may not be as difficult to get a volunteer as it would be to find a permanent replacement.

But what about the question raised in the title of this section? Aside from a forced removal from office, I can imagine any one of a number of reasons to quit. There are a number of personal reasons, like health or family problems, that might incline you to quit. I won't go into those. Let's look at a few that are closer to being in the professional category.

1. You get tired of doing the work, or your spouse gets tired of having you do the work.

There is often a lot of tension that builds up over the years. The head is the focus of a lot of faculty discontent, often undeservedly so, often a corollary of the job. There are many activities that heads do regularly that are distasteful: meetings, handling complaints, acting as a referee in internecine battles. After a few years this may have a cumulative effect. If summers don't renew you and a leave doesn't seem to be a cure, it may be time to resign.

If you have been active in scholarship and begin to slack off, it may be that the job has begun to drain you of the psychic energy that enabled you to maintain your dual career as administrator and researcher. Some symptoms: you wander the halls of the math building looking for something to do or someone to talk to, you begin watching more television, you have trouble sleeping at night, you begin training for the marathon, you decide to write a biography of

Jack Kerouac. Just remember that if you are not enjoying your job as head, it won't be long before others are not enjoying having you as head. It's a lot better to depart with people crying about it than with everyone heaving a sigh of relief.

But before you decide you are too tired of the job, take a vacation. Go to St Jean-Cap-Ferrat, sit in the cafés looking at the sea, blow a wad on lunch at the Chateau de la Chevre d'Or in Eze, have a champagne picnic on Cap Martin. If you still think you are tired of being head, the condition is permanent. Announce your retirement.

2. Your agenda has been realized, at least as far as you think it possible, and you want to get back to writing your book.

Go back to the reason why you became head. After a while you may feel that either you have accomplished what you set out to do or you are never going to reach that goal. If there are no more castles to conquer, it might be time to hang it up. As I said in §5, if you don't have an agenda, don't be a head. So if you are not prepared to pursue some program that will be beneficial to the department and the university, consider resigning. Otherwise the department will begin to sour on you, you will approach brain death, and your return to faculty status will be far more painful.

3. Your ideas no longer mesh well with the dean's.

Again, this goes back to some of the earlier sections that discuss whether you should become a head. If you can't get along with the dean or cannot make your agenda mesh with his/hers, it may be time to go. It may be that the dean has lost confidence in you. Maybe the dean retires and the new dean is a different animal. In any case, if you cannot communicate with your boss, the department will suffer.

Actually, under some such circumstances you might do the department one last service by such a departure. Resigning under protest might be the means of getting the dean to come around to your and the department's point of view. There is a careful road to follow here, and this should be done with caution. Don't be too ready to end your career unless you mean it. Don't expect the faculty to picket the dean's office demanding your return. My experience, not just as a head, is that when you go out on a limb, you are usually there alone.

4. You take another job.

OK, I know, when you go to another university, you resign your present position. In fact I am not going to talk about your entertaining an outside offer. I'll leave the entertaining to you. But let's discuss the possibility that the dean resigns or there is an opening for an associate dean in your own university. There are considerable consequences to your moving in such a direction.

Deciding whether to move into an administrative position that oversees a larger segment of the university deserves a lot of thought. It seems to me that most people who become associate deans retain a strong connection with their home departments. Sometimes it is a part-time position. Associate deans have the ear of the dean and can, therefore, influence educational policy in the college. Some might also see it as a leg up in getting into higher administration.

Associate deans seem to have to do a lot of paperwork (more than deans) and attend a lot of meetings (as many as deans). Yet they do not have the degree of control over their unit that either a dean or a department head has.

Deans have more power than department heads. They can make budget decisions that affect the entire college. One of the drawbacks to being a department head is the lack of control you have over your budget. No matter how hard you work and plan and no matter how ambitious you are, you have to wait until someone (the dean) decides to give you the funds required to carry out your plan. The dean does depend on the campus administration for his/her funds, but the consequences seem different both in size and perspective.

The dean's budget is much larger than a department head's. So if there is .5% of the college budget available for "playing", it is a sizable piece of change and (s)he can do a lot with it. A .5% fudge zone in a department's budget accomplishes far less. Also, the dean is usually less emotionally involved when (s)he requests additional funds from the campus administration for a project. That project originated with a department head who is sweating a lot more over this than the dean.

I also think a dean has less chance to see the direct consequences of his/her decisions. At the very least, the change wrought by one of his/her decisions takes longer to be manifest. Deans hire department heads and a new department head can make a difference in a short time. But the differences are probably more apparent inside the department than in the college office.

All this is conjecture, of course, since I have only observed deans and never experienced the office. But be clear about one thing. When you decide to become a dean, it is a full-time job. You might continue to teach a course in the mathematics department, but your scholarly life will suffer dramatically. This usually means crossing the line from mathematician/administrator to administrator. Be sure this is what you want.

Give appropriate notice.

Finally, when you decide to end it all, allow the department a year to replace you. If your term is short, a semester and a summer might be enough. But a year seems like an optimal time.

Either you will be replaced from within the department or there will be a national search. Clearly a search, replete with advertisements and interviews, is going to take time. If you know there will be a search, it might be advisable to let the dean know even before you announce it to the department. This way (s)he can find the extra money a search will require. But don't tell the dean too soon. You don't want to spend too much time as a lame duck with the dean postponing decisions about the department until your replacement arrives. In fact, there is probably another section needed for this book that would discuss how to act in limbo. But that will have to wait until I experience it.

Even if your replacement is to be one of your present colleagues, (s)he need time. People have to fully consider whether they want the job. The internal politics of the department has to run its course and faculty sentiment must be given time to coalesce around one or two professors. In this case, however, it is probably a good idea that the process should not take too long. Too much politicking might leave scar tissue. Also, you should have some time left to have a transitional period, which might contribute to the department's health.

Then you can sit back, write the book you have been wanting to, go to St Jean-Cap-Ferrat, come back and carp at that damn new head who is screwing up all that you accomplished.